A Living

KATHRYN KUHLMAN:

A Spiritual Biography
of God's Miracle Working Power

A Living Classic Book

KATHRYN KUHLMAN:

A *Spiritual Biography*
of *God's Miracle Working Power*

by
Roberts Liardon

Harrison House
Tulsa, Oklahoma

We would like to express our appreciation to the Kathryn Kuhlman Foundation (P. O. Box 3, Pittsburgh, PA 15230) for their permission to use excerpts from sermons by Kathryn Kuhlman and photographs of her.

Kathryn Kuhlman —
A Spiritual Biography
of God's Miracle Working Power
ISBN 0-89274-562-2
Copyright © 1990 by Roberts Liardon
P. O. Box 23238
Minneapolis, Minnesota 55423

Published by **Harrison House, Inc.**
P. O. Box 35035
Tulsa, Oklahoma 74153

Dedication

*B*ehind every ministry is the support team which holds up the hands of the minister as Aaron and Hur did for Moses. (Exod. 17:12.) I would like to express my appreciation and thanks to those people who loyally served Kathryn Kuhlman and assisted her ministry. Her anointing could not have influenced the world in the magnitude it has without the people who faithfully supported her.

Contents

Introduction

1 A Miracle Service   11

2 The Imprints of Childhood   25

3 Milestones of Spiritual Growth   33

4 The Calling   43

5 The Day Kathryn Kuhlman "Died"   53

6 The First Miracle   61

7 Her Best Friend   75

8 The Glory Belongs to God   83

Appendix I: Biographical Outline   95

Appendix II: Messages by Kathryn Kuhlman   103

     1. The Holy Spirit   103

     2. Radio Messages   113

         "Are You Cashing God's Personal Checks?"   113

         "Release From Depression"   119

         "Love Has Never Yet Made a Sacrifice"   126

         "God's Practical Advice About Love"   133

         "God Demands Sinlessness in Worship"   139

         "Dangers That Beset a Life of Victory"   144

Introduction

"I Believe in Miracles."

*A*fter attending a Kathryn Kuhlman Miracle Service, thousands of people would leave saying, "I believe in miracles also!" What the people of her day saw was out of the ordinary; it was beyond human comprehension.

Kathryn Kuhlman was a woman so dependent and yielded to the Lordship of Jesus Christ that the Holy Spirit had liberty to do as He desired. The miraculous was so evident in her meetings that even the worst skeptic would leave in bewilderment, or as many did, leave believing that Jesus does still live.

We can learn valuable lessons from her life and ministry. Let those of us called to minister in *this* hour walk on the road that Kathryn Kuhlman helped pave — *the road of the miraculous.*

From the time I attended my first Kathryn Kuhlman service as a very young boy, I have been fascinated by her life and ministry. My purpose in writing this book is not to retell the story of her natural life but to draw some spiritual lessons *from* her life.

I have not written a biography, but I have attempted to write of her spiritual odyssey, of what was really happening in the spiritual realm during all of these things that could be seen by the natural eye.

She was a very important person in God's plan for His twentieth-century Church. In a literal sense of the word, she was a "forerunner" of the Church of the future. There was a "prophetic tone" in her ministry that showed what the Church would be like in times to come.

Kathryn Kuhlman laid a world foundation for the workings of the Holy Spirit. Her ministry shifted the focus of the Body of Christ from the supernatural gifts manifested in the Pentecostal movement back to the *Giver of the gifts,* the Holy Spirit.

Kathryn Kuhlman was unique, although she called herself an ordinary person. The word *unique* is overused and misused today, but in a very literal sense, there has been no one else like her. Many have tried to imitate her voice and her theatrical mannerisms but have failed. Many have tried to translate the anointing that was on her into techniques and methods, but that has not been possible. Those attempting to copy her have had no power, no anointing.

Kathryn was a woman of great humility. She was careful to give God *all* of the glory for everything that occurred in her life and ministry. She stated consistently that the healings which occurred through her ministry were not her doing but the work of God. People came forward in her meetings to testify *of* their healings — not to *receive* healing.

I thank God for Kathryn Kuhlman, an example of one who was unafraid to pay the price to walk in His service. I am grateful for the lessons I have learned through her life, and I want to share some of those lessons in this book — many of them in her own words.

Chapter 1:
A Miracle Service

"Why Aren't They All Healed?

*T*he tall, attractive woman in a floor-length, flowing chiffon gown stands motionless at the bottom of four steps that lead up to a platform. Then she begins to move up those steps stopping again on the last one. She walks to a door with a black doorknob. As she has done many times before, she stands with her hand on that black doorknob. In that spot she "dies a thousand deaths," which she does each time she stands there.

She knows people are waiting out there, some in great pain, some making herculean efforts to be there in wheelchairs or on stretchers, some coming from long distances. She knows that without yielding to the Holy Spirit in many "deaths to self," He will not be able to move freely through her to heal these people.

She opens the door, and out she goes, flying as it were, to center stage of Carnegie auditorium. A spiritual current surges through the people seated in the vast auditorium.

There, facing her, sit people from all races, creeds, and religions. They have come from all over the world seeking help from the woman who believes in miracles. Medical science has given up on many of them. They have no hope, having been "sentenced to die" by their conditions or diseases. The last hope of many in the auditorium is to attend a Kathryn Kuhlman Miracle Service. They have heard that here the sick are healed.

Many of them have thought the same thing: "Maybe *I* can obtain a miracle through this woman who believes in them."

Greetings flow from Miss Kuhlman to the vast sea of people. She knows in herself that she could not heal a single one. She never claims to heal anyone. She depends on the unseen Source of her life, her best friend, the Holy Spirit.

From her heart, she shares the truth that she knows so well, as she walks across the stage speaking of the One Whom she trusts beyond human understanding. Tears stream down her cheeks as she looks upward.

She turns and looks at the upper balcony, "Someone is being healed of sugar diabetes," then looking toward the main floor, she points, declaring that asthma is being healed.

"I see the Holy Spirit in this area of the auditorium," and she points to the wheelchair area.

Suddenly, it is happening! It is happening all over the building! People are getting up from wheelchairs and seats amazed, yet in inexpressible happiness. Braces are discarded, wheelchairs abandoned, hearing aids removed forever! These people are healed.

Up on stage they go, in front of the woman who believes in miracles.

"What happened to you?" she asks.

"How do you know?" is her second question.

Those in her vicinity begin to fall backwards, flat on their backs under the power of the Holy Spirit, while thousands cry and laugh with these who are healed.

Several hours later, the service concludes.

There, on stage, stands Miss Kuhlman, crying as they leave. Why is she crying after such a great service?

The reason is that she has seen someone being pushed outside to be taken home, still in his wheelchair. This poor soul has not been healed. She asks why. She is even more disappointed than the person who was not healed.

She walks off the platform, back through the door and back down the four steps wondering if she *did* completely yield to the Holy Spirit. All of her life she will question whether she could have better cooperated with Him, although she yielded to Him and cooperated with Him to a degree few ministers and church leaders have achieved throughout the past two thousand years.

Standing with tears of compassion flowing down her face, she asks a question that she continues to ask — without any answers — all of her life: "Why aren't they all healed?"

* * *

The first time I saw Kathryn Kuhlman was at the Civic Center in Tulsa, Oklahoma, when I was seven years old. The auditorium already was jammed, so we had to sit on the third floor of the center, which I believe has since been torn down to make room for newer construction.

We had to hear her through an intercom system, and I remember her deep voice. Toward the end of the service as people began to leave, we slipped into the auditorium. I remember standing there looking at her up on the stage. I do not remember what she said, but it seemed hundreds of people were in front of the platform — whether for an altar call, to give testimonies of healing, or just to get near her and shake her hand.

Musicians were singing the last song of the service, and we took a good look at her. That sight of her, and the people, and the crowded auditorium is indelibly printed on my memory.

The second time Kathryn Kuhlman came to Tulsa, I was there also, my second time to see her. She visited the Mabee Center on the Oral Roberts University campus, and the building was packed to capacity. The church my family attended had a special section reserved in the balcony.

My mother was part of the special choir for the service. She had gone for a rehearsal some weeks earlier, so my family had talked of this meeting for days. Many of the people from our church also were part of the choir.

I remember all of the wheelchairs I saw. Miss Kuhlman looked like a white speck from where we sat in the balcony, because the auditorium was darkened and a spotlight was on her. She wore a white dress and talked like a little person with a deep voice. Actually, she was tall in height, but when you are up in the balcony looking down, someone on stage appears very small — especially to a youngster.

In the weeks before the meeting, two of my best friends from the church and I talked a lot about all the miracles of which we had heard happened in her services. There was an excitement about the meeting before you ever got there, because testimonies of the miracles and the moving of the Holy Spirit went before her.

When she walked into the building, an expectancy had been built up in the people to receive from God and to hear what He was saying. She talked and introduced some other people, and I do not remember anything about her message. I do remember her weeping a little bit sometime during the sermon.

Then, all of a sudden, she began to have words of knowledge (1 Cor. 12:8), and she began to call people out. I saw some nuns who were there in wheelchairs get up and walk as well as some other people. They got up out of their chairs just as non-handicapped people get up out of their seats, as if there was no hindrance and no problem with rising and walking.

Afterwards, it seemed people were in a kind of ecstasy about that meeting. For days and weeks afterwards, there was talk of those who were healed and of how fantastically God had moved.

The third time she came to Tulsa, I did not attend. However, my mother again was part of the choir and was able to take her mother, who lived with us, into the Mabee Center early and get her a good seat. She wanted to sit close enough to see Miss Kuhlman, but not so close that she had to crane her neck to look up at her.

The thing my grandmother remembers most about Kathryn Kuhlman's appearance is the white gown she wore, and the thing she remembers most about the service is the sight of crippled people walking. All of a sudden, Grandmother says, when sicknesses and diseases were being called out as healed, she heard a rustling, metallic noise. When she turned around, she saw that noise had been the sound of people leaving their wheelchairs.

I asked her, "How many got up and walked? Was it five or six?"

She said, "No, there were *many* who got up and left their wheelchairs!"

So I would estimate at least ten or fifteen. Grandmother said the miracles were things that you could not understand with your natural mind.

The second most vivid thing she remembers about the service is that everyone Kathryn came close to or touched was slain in the Spirit. They fell backwards under the power, even at times, ushers were affected by the power of the Holy Spirit and fell in the aisles.

Also, I remember when I was still a little boy that Grandmother attended a Kathryn Kuhlman crusade in Oklahoma City. Our church chartered a bus and took a number of people. At this meeting, my grandmother came back home talking about the length of the sermon.

Recently, when I talked to her about these meetings, I asked, "Was it a sermon, or just a talk?"

She said, "No, Kathryn never really preached, she just talked."

Miss Kuhlman herself called her sermons "heart-to-heart talks" in which she would share the inner thoughts and impressions of her spirit, as well as truths from the Word. Those talks brought her hearers into a closer knowledge of the realm of the Spirit where she walked. That place was such a reality to her that she was able to make it real to those who heard her with the "listening ears" of the spirit.

Grandmother said she could feel the power of the Holy Spirit move in a tangible way all through the service, from the beginning to the end — just the continual moving of the Holy Spirit. Becoming aware of that realm brought people to a realization that they also could live there, and they reached out for the Holy Spirit.

After she had talked for some time and perhaps cried a little, all of a sudden, the congregation would be in unity with her, and the miracles would begin. When people reached out and became hungry for the kind of relationship she had, this brought miracles to them.

I believe the day will come when we will operate in that same fashion, in a greater demonstration of the miraculous than any we have seen since her day.

An Historic Day in Church Annals

On July 4, 1948, Kathryn Kuhlman held her first "miracle service" at Carnegie Hall in Pittsburgh.

Those services continued for twenty years, and I believe, are the most incredible services since the days of the early apostles.

They started with music. Kathryn always knew the value of music in bringing a crowd into unity of spirit. She always wanted to use really good — if not great — musicians, partly because she enjoyed music. However, she also felt that anything done for the Lord ought to be the best that was available.

Jimmy Miller, a pianist at People's Church, a large church on the north side of Pittsburgh, and Charles Beebee, organist at the same church, were at the instruments in Carnegie Hall for that first service and remained with the Kuhlman ministry until Kathryn died.

In 1952, the director of the Mendelssohn Choir in Pittsburgh — Dr. Arthur Metcalfe — joined Kathryn's services as choir director and remained with her until he died in 1975, one year to the day before her death.

Still later, well-known pianist Dino Kartsonakis joined her ministry and stayed until shortly before her death, and noted baritone Jimmie McDonald was soloist for her services until she died.

From the very first, the services at Carnegie Hall were packed to overflowing. Each service, the place was filled with a sense of expectancy that is indescribable. Of course, the emotions of those attending were affected, and in many people, perhaps the emotions were *all* that were involved. However, the "excitement" in her meetings — or in any meeting where there is the presence of the Holy Spirit — is not initiated in the emotions.

In Kathryn's services, His presence was manifested in a healing anointing which bathed the soul and body in waves of cleansing. Even those who did not receive bodily healing left the meetings, I believe, with healings of wounds and hurts and with the "cares of this world" dropped off, at least temporarily.

Many of those who came to scoff or to criticize were affected as much as those who came expecting to receive. Kathryn talked about the fact that some unbelievers received healing and how those incidents upset her "theology." Only those who had hardened hearts through having resisted the Lord for long periods of time, or whose minds were "programmed" against the supernatural, or who walked in religious traditions were unaffected by the atmosphere in her miracle services. They were like boulders or logs that a fresh-running stream must flow around. They sat like islands in a lake of healing power and were not touched.

On the other hand, for various reasons, not all of those who *were* touched by the presence of the Holy Spirit — or who were aware of the supernatural manifestation — received healing.

The key to understanding her ministry is the way the Holy Spirit chose to manifest. As the group came into unity with her, He flowed outward across the room like a wave of cleansing, healing water. Any disease or condition that *could* be moved was washed away. Only the Lord knows the individual reasons why some of the diseases or conditions were not affected by the wave. However, the root cause of lack of healing did not lie with the Holy Spirit. He was there for all who could receive.

On the other hand, there should never be any condemnation placed on those who are not healed. The cause is between that person and God. This kind of condemnation grieved Kathryn Kuhlman greatly when she saw it as she visited tent meetings of some ministers in the healing revival of the forties.

The person who goes to a meeting expecting healing and does not receive needs love, compassion, and prayer — not judging, criticism, and condemnation. The right attitudes of pastors, family members, and friends may make the difference in that person's receiving healing the next time.

Her understanding that she did not know what the Holy Spirit was doing until He told her kept her from putting Him in a box or from falling into the trap of formulas and methods. This clear knowledge that without Him she could do nothing kept her sensitive to the Holy Spirit, kept her walking close enough to be able to *know* Him.

The Holy Spirit used her as an interpreter of what He had done, rather than as a vessel for His healing power. She told the people what the Holy Spirit was doing, as He told her. She was also an "orchestrator" for what He was doing. Some critics thought Kathryn Kuhlman was deliberately staging her services; however, those who were sensitive to the Holy Spirit knew better.

The presence of the Holy Spirit cannot be faked, staged, or manipulated. Only a genuine desire and respect for His presence will open the door for Him to manifest — and that desire and respect is what Kathryn Kuhlman uniquely had and was able to communicate to her audiences.

As she said many times, and I have pointed out in this book, she was willing to pay the price to be totally used by Him. Therefore He was able to manifest more fully than He can in many services. The Holy Spirit is present within every born-again person. However, His presence was with Kathryn in that full, almost tangible, way whether she was on stage preaching or walking down the street.

Apparently, she had so dealt with desires of the world, desires of the flesh, and "self-rights" that He had fewer "boulders and logs" to flow around in her. That does not mean, of course, that she was perfect. Until she died, the Lord was still working on her as He is on all of us; but, just *think* how God could use any of us who would be willing to give up as much of the self-life as she did.

In the Great Awakening revival, they called this "sanctification." The Apostle Paul called it working out your own salvation. (Phil. 2:12 *KJV*), and he was not talking of salvation of the spirit which brings eternal life. He was talking about areas of the soul and body that retain the old nature of the Satan-overshadowed world instead of being like the new nature of the spirit.

The minute a person is born again, he becomes a house divided against itself. By sovereign grace, He has had the nature of Christ imputed to him. He has had his "dead" spirit brought alive by the impartation of the life of God within him. But his mind, emotions, and body still need to be renewed, conformed to the image of Christ within Him. (Rom. 8:29.)

How do you do this? The same way Kathryn Kuhlman did: Give up those things of "self" which are of the old nature and allow the Holy Spirit the same authority in your mind and emotions and over your body that He has over your spirit. Stop serving two masters; "take up your cross," and follow Jesus. (Matt. 16:24.)

The sign of taking up the cross, or getting on the "cross" to be "crucified and resurrected," is *not my will, but thine be done.* (Luke 22:42.) When you can truly say that to the Lord, the Holy Spirit will have free reign in your life, as He did in hers.

An Atmosphere of Praise and Worship

"Setting the stage" for the appearance of the Holy Spirit cannot be done in natural ways. He will not be "stage-managed."

She set the stage for Him through her own expectancy of His presence. Her dependency on Him drew Him to her.

By not knowing exactly how the Holy Spirit was going to move until He had done it, she was more excited and interested than anyone else in her meetings. Some have said she kept a "girl-like excitement," but really it was child-like faith coupled with her knowledge of all the wonderful things He had done in all the services before. Sensitivity to His presence, a child-like faith that He would come and do good things, and past knowledge of His goodness and mercy kept her always walking out onto that stage with an almost electric sense of expectancy.

One woman described in the following words how Kathryn operated:[1]

> All the things I had been taught about healing I had to unlearn in Kathryn's meetings as it was always a new approach...She interviewed each person as if it were the first time she had seen a miracle. She always was excited about the healings and (her excitement) inspired faith....
>
> She constantly gave all the glory to God for the healings. She knew she was not a "faith healer." The minute she walked on the stage, she created a beautiful atmosphere of praise and worship. This, too, inspired faith. You could feel the presence of many angels who assisted Kathryn in her meetings. Only God knows the secret and the full impact of her ministry.
>
> Kathryn was a born organizer. She was like a spiritual general in the Lord's army. Her ushers were trained, one by one, to handle problems and emergencies. The choir had a special director to

---

[1]Hosier, Helen Kooiman. *Kathryn Kuhlman The Life She Led, The Legacy She Left,* (Old Tappan: Fleming H. Revell Company, 1976), p. 125.

prepare them for ministry. Lady advisors were taught to be led by the Holy Spirit. Workers were assigned to a special area, so all the audience could be ministered to.

Much of her direction came from the Holy Spirit as her ministry developed; however, her character had been formed during childhood. And much of her behavior was an outgrowth of those character traits.

Chapter 2:

The Imprints
of Childhood

"Train up a child in the way he should go;
and when he is old,
he will not depart from it."
Proverbs 22:6 KJV

*T*he things we learn in our early formative years shape the rest of our lives.

The "imprints of childhood" for Kathryn included a permissive father, whose attitude was her measurement for those who loved her for the rest of her life; a stern, strict disciplinarian mother; a lack of formal education — her last schooling apparently was the tenth grade; and an appearance that was not appealingly feminine during her adolescent years.

However, the relationship with her father instilled in her a trust in male authority that allowed her to trust God the Father easier than many Christians can. She drew this conclusion herself in one of her sermons:[1]

---

[1]Sermon by Kathryn Kuhlman. "Correct Praying Is Your Faith Being Voiced." (Used by permission of the Kathryn Kuhlman Foundation, Pittsburgh, PA.)

In the 6th chapter of Matthew, we call it "the Lord's Prayer," but it isn't really the Lord's prayer. It is the prayer the Lord Jesus taught us to pray. . . .

If you find it hard to pray, it's because you have never really recognized this wonderful relationship. Do you say it is the most difficult thing in the world for you to come in the presence of your earthly parent and converse with him?

Maybe this (relationship) is so real to me because of my relationship with Papa. If you know me well, you know that of all human beings I have known, my relationship with Papa was the greatest. Oh! I would hang on him. I would love him.

Mama would say to me, "Stop hanging on Papa!"

Dear me, he was carrying me when my legs were so long they would drag on the pavement. He would no sooner hang up his coat when he got home — before he even had a chance to wash his hands and comb his hair — I would be hanging on him. He would sit down — oh, poor papa — to rest a minute, and I was all over him, my arms around his neck, yakking, chatting, never shutting my mouth, my words coming so fast.

And Mama would say, "Can't you be quiet? Papa's tired. Just sit down, and be quiet."

I had to tell Papa everything. I knew Papa wanted to know. There wasn't a thing that happened that day (that I did not tell Papa). There never was a person easier for me to converse with than Papa. To this day, and Papa's been gone a long time, there are things that I wish I could run and tell Papa.

That's why this relationship with our heavenly Father is just as real and just as personal. I never memorized anything to tell Papa. It came so spontaneously. And that's the way it is with our heavenly Father. "Our *Father* which art in heaven". . . (Matt. 6:9 KJV).

There must be the knowledge of that relationship between yourself and your heavenly Father, and when you talk to Him, you must be conscious of His power — not only that, but that He's concerned about every detail in that life of yours.

Her Father lived and died without ever having punished her once. Her mother was the one who disciplined her. Perhaps Emma Kuhlman overcompensated for the father's lack of discipline. Kathryn said:[2]

> He never laid his hands on me. Never. Not once. Mama was the one who disciplined me. I got it down in the basement so the neighbors could not hear me scream.
>
> Then, when Papa came home, I would run to him, sit on his lap, and he would take away all the pain. I can never remember, as a child, having my mother show me any affection. Never. Mama was a perfect disciplinarian. But she never once told me she was proud of me or that I did well. Never once. It was Papa who gave me the love and affection.

Kathryn's father, Joseph Kuhlman, never understood his wife's harsh disciplining of the children. Their one son, Kooley, left home young; an older daughter, Myrtle, married young, and Kathryn went to live with Myrtle at 16.

When Joe tried to interfere with Emma's spankings and frequent criticism of Kathryn, she turned on *him*. Joe began spending more time away from home as the children grew up and finally fixed up a small room in back of his livery stable where he frequently spent the night. In those years before Kathryn left home, he began to take her with him when he collected bills owed to his stable. The merchants called her "little Joe."

---

[2]Jamie Buckingham. *Kathryn Kuhlman Daughter of Destiny* (Plainfield: Logos International. Copyright 1976), p. 15.

From her father's competent business practices, Kathryn learned things that shaped her attitude toward sound business principles in ministry.

A Heritage of Thriftiness and Hard Work

Concordia was settled by German immigrants, who began arriving in the late 1830s, although the town was not named until 1865. Kathryn's ancestors on both sides were hardy people with tremendous self-discipline. They were hard-working people and proud of their background. Those traits of hard work and self-discipline were among the influences of childhood that shaped Kathryn Kuhlman's life.

She said once:[3]

In Concordia, Missouri, if you got up in the morning, and you didn't feel good, do you know what those German Lutheran folk did? They went out and worked.

My Papa would say, "Well, work it off, honey. Just work it off."

And Mama used to say, "That's all right, honey. You just take the scrub brush, and you start scrubbing the sidewalks. It won't be long until you'll feel better."

Well, even the thoughts of that scrub brush cured me so fast, it wasn't even funny!

The attitude and inclination toward hard work was ingrained in her throughout her entire life. In those early years, that attitude was reflected in her diligence and perseverence in

---

[3]Sermon by Kathryn Kuhlman. "Knowing How To Have Power Over Difficulties." (Used by permission of the Kathryn Kuhlman Foundation.)

studying the Word. Sometimes she wondered what she might have missed through working so hard:[4]

> It seems that all I have done is preach and pray, and work and pray some more, preach some more, and work a little harder. Sometimes I wonder if I have missed anything by not having the same kind of youth that thousands of young people have had. All I've known — few people realize it — but all of my life has been nothing but hard work.

> You wonder why I know the Word of God as I do. It is because, since I can remember, I've searched the Scripture. I've been hungry for the Word of God. I have sought understanding of the things that are spiritual. It seems all I have done is pray one constant prayer, being constantly conscious of His presence. That is the reason He is as real to me as the next beat of my heart — more real to me, very, very often, than one sitting in the room with me.

Kathryn's mother, Emma Walkenhorst, married Joseph Kuhlman in 1891, and Kathryn was born May 9, 1907, on their farm about five miles from Concordia, according to her permanent high school record. (Birth certificates were not required by Missouri until 1910.) When she was about two, Joe sold the 160-acre farm and built a big house in town, a house that Kathryn always called home. In fact, she loved it so much that she insisted on having been born in that house, although the facts are otherwise.

She was named — with a different spelling — after her father's mother, Catherine Marie Sahrragen Borgstedt, whose first husband died in Germany. Catherine Marie married John

---

[4]Kuhlman Sermon. "Guidelines for Life's Greatest Virtue." (Used by permission of Kathryn Kuhlman Foundation.)

Henry Kuhlman in 1851, and they migrated to Concordia in 1853. This great-grandmother was noted for her hard work, spinning wool for the whole neighborhood. She also was subject to epileptic seizures.[5] Kathryn's middle name, Johanna, was for her maternal grandmother, (Hannah) Kuester Walkenhorst.

A childhood friend described young Kathryn this way:[6]

> . . . Large features, red hair, and freckles. It could not be said of Kathryn that she was pretty. She wasn't dainty or appealingly feminine in any sense of the word. She was taller than the rest of "our gang" (five feet eight), gangly and boyish in build, and her long strides kept the rest of us puffing to keep up with her.
>
> Her manner was rather brash instead of ladylike, and I daresay she often tried the patience of her mother who was apt to be more rigid and inflexible in her views.

Kathryn also was noted as a young girl for her "independence and self-reliance and desire to do things her way."[7]

Rough Waters and Deep Seas

Things that have happened in any of our lives can be beneficial, if we will surrender to God and commit our lives totally to His use. Because Kathryn "died to self" and rose to serve God, she developed a will that was never broken by her mother's harsh discipline, a personal integrity that extended to her finances in the ministry, and a dedication to God's work that brought her into an unusual relationship with the Holy Spirit.

---

[5]Obituary in the German Family Bible, Jan. 28, 1907.

[6,7]Hosier, p. 38.

When she was only seventeen, she wrote three wise sentences down in a little red book, apparently some sort of diary or blank notebook. Years later, she picked up that little book and reread those words.

Whether life grinds a man down or polishes him depends on what he's made of.

A diamond cannot be polished without friction nor man perfected without trials.

Great pilots are made in rough waters and deep seas.

When I closed the book an hour ago, I turned back the pages of my life. Years have come, and years have gone since the day I wrote those words, and I can bear witness to the fact that every word of it I wrote that day is true.

I feel I am the person that I am today because of those deep waters. Not the sunshine in my life, but the storms, the winds, the gales (have polished me). And I'll say it to you without fear of contradiction. It is true. Friend, these things come into your life. It depends on what you're made of whether you permit them to defeat you or whether you use them for the glory of God.

. . . I can turn back the pages of my life, and there *are* certain milestones. I can put my finger on them. I know exactly the day, the hour, when I could have gone down in defeat. I know the places, I know the times, I know the cities, I know the happenings, I know the crises in my life when I could have put up that white flag of defeat. I could have gone down and been defeated by self-pity.

I wouldn't be where I am this very hour had it not been for the disappointments, had it not been for the storms, but I made up my mind I wasn't going to be one of those little birds that run for shelter the first time the winds start to blow.[8]

---

[8]Sermon, "Knowing How To Have Power Over Difficulties."

Her emphasis on self-reliance may sound contradictory to her emphasis on "dying to self"; however, the two things are not contradictory. She also said, in the same message:

I could not have done it in myself, but when I made the effort, God was there to help me. When you pray, you get into the stream of power — His power. All you have to do is yield yourself to God, ask Him to take care of you. Ask Him to take care of those things in your life that are bigger than you, and you'll soon find yourself being lifted above all obstacles, all storms, all difficulties.

There were some big milestones in her life before she ever reached adulthood. Among them were leaving home in her teens to travel with her sister and brother-in-law in a tent ministry and then beginning her own ministry.

Chapter 3:

Milestones of Spiritual Growth

"Paying the price is never a one-time experience."

*T*he first big milestone in her life came when she was about fourteen years old: It was her conversion. She told the story many times in her life. She answered what seems to be almost a sovereign wooing of the Holy Spirit — not through any person. She came from a "religious" background rather than a spiritual one, and the churches she attended never gave altar calls.

When telling of her conversion, Kathryn said:[1]

I was standing beside Mama, and the hands of the church clock were pointed to five minutes before twelve o'clock noon. I can't remember the minister's name or even one word of his sermon, but something happened to me. It's as real to me right now as it was then — the most real thing that ever happened to me.

As I stood there, I began shaking to the extent that I could no longer hold the hymnal, so I laid it on the

---

[1]Hosier, pp. 32,33.

pew . . . and sobbed. I was feeling the weight of (conviction) and I realized that I was a sinner. I felt like the meanest, lowest person in the whole world. Yet I was only a fourteen-year-old girl.

Altar calls were never given in that little Methodist church. I had often seen them take in new church members, but this was much different for me! I did the only thing I knew to do: I slipped out from where I was standing and walked to the front pew and sat down in the corner of the pew and wept. Oh, how I wept!

. . .Then the recognition came over Kathryn's young being that this was an occasion for joy. (She said) . . . I had become the happiest person in the whole world. The heavy weight had lifted. I experienced something that has never left me. I had been born again, and the Holy Spirit had done the very thing that Jesus said He would do: (John 16:8).

Attending church was as much a part of life as work during Kathryn's years in Concordia. However, she was of a split-denominational family. She was attending the Methodist Church with her mother about 1921 when she was born again, in spite of the fact that her mother had been removed from membership there when she married Joe Kuhlman, a Baptist. However, the entire family is listed from 1922 as members of the Baptist Church, and in 1958, Emma Kuhlman's funeral was held in the Baptist Church.[2]

Kathryn several times mentioned in her sermons that her Grandpa Walkenhorst was of the firm conviction that the only people who would ever make heaven would be Methodists!

---

[2]Skogen, Larry C., *Kathryn Kuhlman: A Bio-Bibliography,* Central Missouri State University, Warrensburg, Missouri, July 31, 1984.

However, she also added that her grandfather did not know one thing about being born again.

"If Grandpa Walkenhorst did make heaven — I'm not so sure he did — but if he did, he got the shock of his life when he found some Baptists there," she said.[3] In the same service, she said her grandfather practically disowned her mother when she married a Baptist.

Her mother taught Epworth League meetings for young people at the Methodist Church in Kathryn's teen years. A neighbor said Mrs. Kuhlman was an "excellent Bible teacher, and Kathryn and her sisters and brother must have received some very fine teaching and training at home." The neighbor also talked of hearing someone in the Kuhlman family singing in the evenings and someone else playing the piano.[4]

In spite of her mother's being well-versed in the Bible and "an excellent teacher," apparently *she* was not born again until 1935 in one of Kathryn's meetings in Denver.

Kathryn's life shows that, like so many other great leaders of the Church in our century, God chooses whom to raise up in a particular ministry. His spiritually great leaders are not made by man, but raised up sovereignly by God and usually perfected through those struggles and storms she talked about.

Oral Roberts, Lester Sumrall, and Kenneth E. Hagin all were raised from death beds and have gone through many

---

[3]"An Hour With Kathryn Kuhlman," Full Gospel Business Men's Fellowship International, Washington, D.C.

[4]Hosier, p. 44.

storms and much persecution, yet their commitment to follow the call of God on their lives has never been shaken.

Kathryn's father died without ever hearing her preach, so when her Denver Revival Tabernacle was established, she invited her mother to visit and attend some of the services. After the close of the first meeting which her mother attended, Kathryn went into the prayer room behind the pulpit to pray for those who answered the invitation.

A few minutes later, her mother also walked into the prayer room and said she wanted to know Jesus as Kathryn knew him.[5]

> Kathryn, now choked with tears, reached out and laid her hand on the back of her mama's head. The moment her fingers touched, mama began to shake, then cry. It was the same kind of shaking and crying that Kathryn remembered when she had stood beside mama in that little Methodist church in Concordia. But this time there was something new. Mama lifted her head and began to speak, slowly at first, then more rapidly. But the words were not English, they were the clear, bell-tone sounds of the unknown tongue.
>
> Kathryn fell to her knees beside her, weeping and laughing at the same time . . .When Emma opened her eyes, she reached out for Kathryn and held her tightly. It was the first time that Kathryn could ever remember being embraced by her mother.

Her mother did not sleep for three days and two nights after that. She was a new person, Kathryn said, and for the rest of her life in Concordia, Emma Kuhlman had a wonderful, sweet communion with the Holy Spirit.

---

[5]Buckingham, pp. 70,71.

That experience must have brought some healing to Kathryn. However, she apparently was concerned that her beloved father might not have been born again. At times, she would speak firmly as if she had no question but that he was with God, but privately at least once, she expressed frustration at not knowing for sure.

She did talk about the fact that her father had an aversion to preachers. Actually, she put it much stronger: Joe Kuhlman despised and hated preachers! In fact, she would say, if he saw a preacher coming down the street, he would cross the street to keep from speaking to him. He thought all preachers were "in it for the money."[6] The only time he attended church was holidays or special services when Kathryn was giving a recitation. As far as she knew, he never prayed or read the Bible.

Kathryn's father was standing in the kitchen when she got home from church that Sunday noon of her conversion, and she ran to tell him her news just as she had run to tell him everything that happened to her in all the years before.

As she told the story, she rushed up to him and said, "Papa, Papa, Jesus has just come into my heart."[7]

Without any emotion, he just said, "Baby, I'm glad, I'm glad."

She was never sure whether he really understood what she meant or not. However, she chose to join her father's Baptist church rather than her mama's Methodist. Even then, she had a mind of her own.[8]

---

[6]"An Hour With Kathryn Kuhlman."

[7]"An Hour With Kathryn Kuhlman."

[8]Buckingham, p. 24.

Milestone Number Two: Leaving Home

Another characteristic of those used greatly by God is their willingness to drop everything and follow His leading. In 1913, her older sister Myrtle had married a young, good-looking evangelist just finishing his course at Moody Bible Institute. Myrtle and Everett Parrott had an evangelistic tent ministry, and in 1923, when Kathryn was 16, she and Myrtle persuaded their parents that it was God's will for her to travel with them.

The Parrotts at that time were headquartered in Oregon. They had become acquainted with a well-known teacher and evangelist, Dr. Charles S. Price, who had a healing ministry and who had introduced them to the baptism in the Holy Spirit. However, almost from the first, the Parrotts' marriage had not been happy, and having the added strain of Kathryn to feed and house apparently did not help matters any.

It would have been easy for her to get into self-pity about this time. She took over the washing on Monday (a household schedule she called her mother's "religion") and ironing on Tuesday. The ironing included the white starched shirts her brother-in-law wore to preach in, and the iron was the heavy metal one of the time that had to be heated over a wood or coal stove — not an easy task.

Among the lessons of patience in adversity that she was learning, lessons that served her well in later years, she also learned not to give way to self-pity.

Many of her later messages flowed out of her personal spiritual growth. A story she told of a woman whose self-centeredness and self-pity had ruined her life and the lives of those around her illustrates the fact that Kathryn learned well that self-pity is a destroyer.[9]

Her life was jammed up, and she brought it all on herself — that awful self-centeredness. Had she pulled out that key log ...of self-centeredness and self-pity, had she changed her center from herself to God, the whole thing would have been cleansed and released.

That was one woman that no one ever heard say, "I'm sorry." Be careful of the person, whether they're a member of your family, whether you work with them, whether they are an employee, be careful of a person who cannot say, "I am sorry." You will find that person very self-centered.

As near as this woman came to it was to say one day, "I'm sorry I did not take better care of my health." Even then, her repentance had a self-reference to it. She was clogged up. She had tied the hands of both God and man. God cannot help her. Her husband cannot help her.

That is the reason you have heard me say ten thousand times that the only person Jesus cannot help, the only person for whom there is no forgiveness of sins is the person who will not say, "I'm sorry for my sins."

...Such a self-centered person usually draws disease to themselves like a magnet.

Kathryn apparently determined while she was a teenager not to allow self-pity or self-centeredness to have a place in her life, no matter what happened to her. Her decision to act on the divinely revealed wisdom of God enabled her to walk on to the next milestone.

---

[9]Sermon by Kathryn Kuhlman. "Not Doing What We Like, But Liking What We Have To Do." (Used by permission of the Kathryn Kuhlman Foundation.)

Her life has shown me that every Christian who will study the Word and pray will have the principles of God revealed to them just as Kathryn Kuhlman did. She always said everyone could have the operation of the Holy Spirit in their lives the way she did — *if they were only willing to pay the price.*

"Paying the price" is not a one-time experience. It begins with an initial commitment and an act of determination to begin a lifetime of paying the price. Part of the price for a spiritual walk that allows the Holy Spirit free reign in your life is the recognition of God's principles when they are brought to your attention — principles such as not allowing self-centeredness to operate in you — *and* the decision to deal with it.

The way to eliminate self-centeredness is found in the Lord's statements to the Pharisees about the greatest commandments:

> Jesus replied: " 'Love the Lord your God with all your heart and with all your soul and with all your mind.'
>
> "This is the first and greatest commandment.
>
> "And the second is like it, Love your neighbor as yourself.
>
> "All the Law and the Prophets hang on these two commandments."
>
> Matthew 22:37-40

In the Charismatic move, we call keeping these two commandments "walking in love." Kathryn Kuhlman learned early in her life that self-centeredness with all the other "self" sins — self-pity, self-indulgence, even self-hatred (judging and condemning oneself) — hinder the Holy Spirit.

There were many other milestones in her life, many other times and places where she could have chosen not to submit to the lessons to be learned through adversity or the growth to be gained through correction from the Holy Spirit. However, fortunately for the Church of Jesus Christ in the twentieth century, she made the right choices.

Chapter 4:

The Calling

"My heart is fixed. I'll be loyal to Him
at any cost, at any price."

*K*athryn never understood why God had
chosen her. She felt there were millions better equipped
for ministry. God took her "nothing" which she offered
up to Him and used it to His glory.

Many critics in the days when her ministry won
worldwide renown never saw her humility and love.
They misunderstood her delivery and personal style and
never looked beneath the mannerisms to the real person.
Previously published biographies about her show that
the mannerisms and style of delivery were not "put on"
but a part of the real Kathryn Kuhlman.

She never accepted the labels that people tried to
attach to her. She emphatically resisted such things as
being called a "faith healer."[1]

All I know is that I'm somebody who loves the Lord
with all my heart.

Hosier, pp. 45, 46.

. . . I resent being called that (faith healer) more than anything. I am just an ordinary person. I really don't know what I am other than just somebody who loves people and wants to try to help everybody that I can. I'm not a faith healer, because I've never healed anyone. It's just the mercy of God.

(Yet she never doubted her calling.) If everybody in the world told me that as a woman I have no right to preach the Gospel, it would have no effect upon me whatsoever, because my call to the ministry was as definite as my conversion.

She called herself "God's handmaiden" — "and on my handmaidens I will pour out in those days of my Spirit; and they shall *prophesy*" (Acts 2:18 KJV). She was using *prophesy* in the sense of telling the good news, or preaching, not in the sense of "foretelling" — which is the current meaning usually applied to that word.

She said a number of times that she did not believe she was God's first choice for the ministry she had, nor even God's second or third choice. She believed all her life that God had called some man to carry forth the work He did through her, and that man was not willing to pay the price. Because she did respond to the call, she inspired people to take their places in God.

Laying a Foundation for Ministry

Kathryn's five years with her sister and brother-in-law were when God laid the foundation for the ministry He wanted to accomplish through her. She not only worked in the household to pick up any burden that her presence might have brought, but she used those years to spend many hours reading and studying the Word.

Without a knowledge and a revelation of the Word, no one called of God can truly answer his or her calling.

In 1928, the Parrotts arrived in Boise, Idaho, with their tent. However, their marital problems had continued to grow, so Everett took the tent and went on to South Dakota while Myrtle, Kathryn, and Helen stayed to hold the scheduled meeting in the Boise Women's Club.

After two weeks, the offerings had not even brought in enough to pay the rent on the building, or their small apartment, or to buy much food. They lived on bread and tuna.[2]

Myrtle felt her only recourse was to rejoin her husband, but the Parrott's pianist, Helen Gulliford, balked. A concert pianist, who at one time had played for Dr. Charles Price's meetings, she felt enough was enough! Kathryn also could not see any hope for the future by continuing to travel with the Parrotts.

Kathryn and Helen decided to cut loose from tent evangelism when a local pastor in Boise offered them a chance to preach in a small pool hall converted into a mission. That was the beginning of the Kathryn Kuhlman Ministry.

From the mission, they went to Pocatello, Idaho, where Kathryn preached in an old opera house, which had to be cleaned before they could use it. Then they went to Twin Falls, Idaho, in the dead of winter. Kathryn slipped on the ice and broke her leg but insisted on preaching in a cast, although the doctor told her not to set foot on the ground for two weeks.

---

[2]All facts concerning those years are based on Buckingham's *Daughter of Destiny,* Chapter III.

She never allowed her flesh to cause her to compromise her obedience to God's will.

Sold on the Things of God

In a sermon once, she said:[3]

The things of God are real to me. I can never remember what folk call backsliding, or ever having the slightest desire to leave the things of God, or to ever stop preaching, or to take (life) a little easier.

My heart is fixed, and when at the age of fourteen, I was born again in that little Methodist church in Concordia, Missouri, my heart became fixed on the things of God, and I've never compromised for one second.

From that first sermon I preached in Idaho — Zacchaeus up a tree, and God knows if anyone was up a tree, I sure was — one thing I knew, I was sold on the things of God. Jesus was real to me. My heart was fixed.

She would humorously tell how after preaching four or five sermons, she felt there was nothing left to preach about![4]

I was walking down the road on my way back to the room where I spent the night, and I wondered, "What more can I preach about? There isn't anything else in the Bible. I have absolutely exhausted the supply of sermons. For the life of me, I can't think of anything else to preach about."

One family with whom she stayed in those years did not have any place for her to stay, so they scrubbed out the turkey house. Kathryn would have slept on a straw stack, she said, because of the need to preach that rose up inside of her. Often, she would laugh

---

[3]Sermon. "Guidelines for Life's Greatest Virtue."
[4]*Heart to Heart With Kathryn Kuhlman,* The Kathryn Kuhlman Foundation, Pittsburgh, PA 15230, 1983, p. 58.

and say that in those early meetings, if she felt anyone there was not saved, she would lock the doors and not let them out. That was her joke; however, she would stay at the altar until the wee hours of the morning and pray with anyone who lingered.

Other places the two girls stayed in Idaho during the winters of the early thirties may have been cleaner and more comfortable than the turkey house, but they were not any warmer. Guest rooms were not heated in those days, and years later she would tell of snuggling under a great pile of covers until she got the place warm where she lay. Then she would turn over on her stomach and study the Word for hours at a time.

Her heart was "sold out" to the Lord, fixed on the things of God. A secret of her ministry was that her heart *was* fixed on Jesus. She was determined to be loyal to Him and not to grieve the Holy Spirit.

In these early years of ministry, we can see two other characteristics develop in her: dedication and loyalty to God and to His people.

She expanded and developed from that early foundation, but she never changed or deviated from the way she understood God's calling on her life during those first years of her ministry.

The Nicest Compliment

She said once:[5]

The nicest compliment that has been paid me for a long time was when someone wrote recently, and they had been in those

---

[5]*See Foonote #3.*

early services when I was so very young, so very inexperienced . . . and said:

"I heard you recently from the Shrine Auditorium, and you haven't changed in your preaching one bit from the time I heard you as a teenager. You've never added any of the rick-a-brick, you've never changed in your theology, you've never gone off on tangents, you've never resorted to fanaticism."

No, beloved. Why should I? I've had the greatest teacher a person can know, the Holy Spirit.

. . . Without (loyalty) life simply falls to pieces. We've gotten to a place where there's so little of loyalty left. Loyalty to each other. Loyalty to what we believe. Loyalty to principles. Loyalty to the Lord Jesus Christ.

That word *loyalty* has little meaning in these days because there's so little of it being practiced.

. . . Loyalty is something that is intangible. It's like love. You can only understand it as you see it in action. . . . *Love is something you do,* and that's also true of loyalty. It means faithfulness. It means allegiance. It means devotion. It means so many, many things.

. . . When we say we're loyal to God, we mean that we believe in His presence, we believe He is the creator, He is the sustainer, the redeemer of our lives. It means we determine to let this faith be the distinctive thing about our own lives as well our relationships with others.

. . . My heart is fixed. I'll be loyal to Him at any cost, at any price. The waters have been deep, and I would not tell you there have not been temptations. I would deceive you if I told you it was an easy way or an easy life. But I also want you to know that I've never been disappointed in Him, never once.

Loyalty is much more than a casual interest in someone or something. It's a personal commitment. In the final analysis, it means, "Here I am. You can count on me. I won't fail you."

As a result of this conviction of the importance of loyalty, she commanded the same sort of loyalty from those closest to her in the ministry. The loyalty of her associates is just as strong today as it was when she was alive.

Faith in a Big God

Kathryn Kuhlman preached faith in a big God. She said if you are serving a God limited in finances, then you are serving the wrong god. Faith towards God was another principle by which she lived.

After preaching all over Idaho, Kathryn and Helen moved on into Colorado. Following a six-month revival in Pueblo, they arrived in Denver. A businessman, Earl F. Hewitt, had joined her in Pueblo as her business manager. That year of 1933 the Depression was in full swing with businesses closed down, millions of people out of work, and churches struggling to stay open.

Traveling evangelists without denominational headquarters to rely on were in even worse plights than ordinary churches. Yet Kathryn had her belief fixed on a big God, whose resources were not limited.

She told Hewitt to go into Denver and act as if they had a million dollars. When he pointed out that in reality they only had $5, she said:[6]

> He's not limited to what we have or who we are. If He can use somebody like me to bring souls into the kingdom, He can certainly use our five dollars and multiply it just as easily as He multiplied the loaves and fishes for the people on the hillside.

[6]Buckingham, p. 57.

Now go on up to Denver. Find me the biggest building you can. Get the finest piano available for Helen. Fill the place up with chairs. Take out a big ad in the *Denver Post* and get spot announcements on all the radio stations. This is God's business, and we're going to do it God's way — big!

Hewitt took her at her word and somehow followed instructions. The building, like the one in Pueblo, had been a Montgomery Ward Company warehouse. The meeting lasted five months, during which time they moved to yet another warehouse.

People were hungry for the Word, although her main message in those years was one of salvation. Pastors were born again at her invitations from time to time. Hers was a ministry of hope and of faith in God that things would get better with the economy and the country.

Helen Gulliford had formed a choir of one hundred voices and composed much of the music they sang. People attended by the hundreds. So when Kathryn announced that the meeting was over, the people would not hear of it. One man offered to make the down payment on a permanent building and erect a huge neon sign over it which would say, "Prayer Changes Things."

A building was found, and renovation was started on it in February of 1934. On May 30 of that year, Denver Revival Tabernacle opened with the huge sign over it as promised. Thousands attended over the next four years. Even people belonging to area churches attended, because services were held every night except Monday.

Started as a revival center, the tabernacle soon developed into a church — simply one without the name and without a denominational affiliation. Soon there was a Sunday school and buses were operated to bring people to services. There were outreaches to prisons and old-folks' homes.

Kathryn, who had been ordained as a Baptist under the Evangelical Church Alliance in Joliet, Illinois, during those years with the Parrotts, conducted weddings and funerals. However, work on the tabernacle was never really finished. In 1938, Kathryn faced one of the hardest trials of her life.

Chapter 5:

The Day Kathryn Kuhlman "Died"

"This was the first time the power of the risen, resurrected Christ came through to me."

*I*n late December 1934, a couple of months before the building to house the Denver Revival Tabernacle was purchased, Kathryn experienced the first real tragedy in her life: Her beloved father was killed in an accident. He had fallen on an icy street or been struck by a car that swerved to try to miss him in a snowstorm. It was never determined for certain what really happened.

Because phone lines were down, it was hours later before a friend could reach Kathryn in Colorado. She started home, driving from Denver across Kansas toward Missouri, with the snowstorm still at blizzard conditions. She said only God knew how fast she drove on icy roads and in near-zero visibility. At Kansas City, she called home to have them tell her father that she was almost there — only to find that he had remained in a coma and died early that morning, December 30, two days after the accident.

What seemed like an unending time later, in the early hours of the next morning, she arrived home to find Papa laid out in his casket in the living room with mourners sitting up to keep the traditional vigil. As she told it to an interviewer more than thirty-five years later, hate welled up inside her toward the youth who had been driving the car.

She said:[1]

> I had always been a happy person, and Papa had helped to make me happy. Now he was gone, and in his place, I was battling unfamiliar strangers of fear and hate.

In 1971, she told a magazine interviewer:[2]

> I had the most perfect father a girl ever had. In my eyes, Papa could do no wrong. He was my ideal. He never spanked me. He never had to. All he had to do was get a certain look on his face. Mama wouldn't hesitate to punish me when I needed it. But Papa punished by letting me know I had hurt him — and that hurt worse than any of my mother's spankings.

She had been gone from home more than ten years with only a few visits in between. Travel was expensive and time-consuming in the Twenties and Thirties. Now Papa would never be able to hear her preach. Later, she related that she had spewed out venom over the accident to everyone she spoke to, and hatred seethed within her until the day of the funeral.[3]

> Sitting there in the front row of the little Baptist church, I still refused to accept my father's death. It couldn't be. My papa, so full of love for his "baby," so tender and gentle, it couldn't be that he was gone.
>
> After the sermon, the townspeople left their pews and solemnly walked down the aisle to gaze one last time into the casket. Then they were gone. The church was empty except for the family and attendants.

[1,2]Hosier, p. 62,60.

One by one, my family rose from their seats and filed by the coffin. Mama. My two sisters. My brother. Only I was left in the pew.

The funeral director walked over and said, "Kathryn, would you like to see your father before I close the casket?"

Suddenly I was standing at the front of the church, looking down — my eyes fixed not on Papa's face, but on his shoulder, that shoulder on which I had so often leaned. I remembered the last conversation we had had. We were in the back yard ....he was standing beside the clothesline, reaching up with his hand on the wire.

"Baby," he said, "When you were a little girl, remember how you used to snuggle your head on my shoulder and say, 'Papa, give me a nickel?'"

I nodded, "And you always did."

"Because it was what you asked for. But, baby, you could have asked for my last dollar, and I would have given you that too."

I leaned over and gently put my hand on that shoulder in the casket. And as I did, something happened. All that my fingers caressed was a suit of clothes. Not just the black wool coat, but everything that box contained was simply something discarded, loved once, laid aside now. Papa wasn't there.

. . .This was the first time the power of the risen, resurrected Christ really came through to me. Suddenly I was no longer afraid of death; and as my fear disappeared, so did my hate. It was my first real healing experience. Papa wasn't dead. He was alive. There was no longer any need to fear or hate.

From this experience, apparently she felt her father was with the Lord, yet she told an interviewer in 1973 that not knowing

---

[3]Ibid, pp. 63,64.

whether he was born again was one of the great frustrations of her life.[4]

Kathryn dated her understanding of death and her compassion for other people's sorrow and grief from that moment at her father's funeral.[5]

> That was many years ago. Since then, I have been able to stand at the open grave with countless others and share the hope that lives in me. There have been mountaintops across those years, opportunities for travel and ministry and preaching. But, you know, growth has come not on the mountaintops but in the valleys. That was the first valley — the deepest — the one that meant most.

Growth Comes in the Valleys

Although she termed the death of her father the "deepest" valley, the next one must have been a close second.

In 1937, among the evangelists, musicians, and preachers who were invited to speak at Denver Revival Tabernacle was a Texas evangelist named Burroughs A. Waltrip. An extremely handsome man, he was eight years older than Kathryn, who even then would not divulge her correct age.

The problem, however, was not his age or his looks — it was the fact that he was married with two little boys. Some eighteen months after his first visit to Denver, he divorced his wife and opened a revival center in Mason City, Iowa, called Radio Chapel, from which he made daily broadcasts over a local radio station.

---

[4]Buckingham, p. 64.
[5]Hosier, p. 64.

Waltrip represented himself there as a single man, and Kathryn Kuhlman and Helen Gulliford came into town to help him raise funds for the chapel. Helen and other friends from Denver tried to talk Kathryn out of marrying the handsome evangelist, but she insisted that his wife had left him which made him free to marry. Whether he deserted his wife or she left him is not certain.

What *is* certain is that Kathryn and Burroughs were married in Mason City on October 18, 1938. What also is certain is that the work she had built so dedicatedly over the previous five years disintegrated. Hewitt bought out her share of the building; Helen resigned and went to help a smaller work in Denver, and the sheep scattered here and there very quickly.

Kathryn spent the next eight years in oblivion as far as major ministry was concerned. Six years were spent in the marriage and the next two trying to find her way back to full-time ministry. Friends who traveled to Mason City during the first few years said she would sit on the platform behind her husband and weep while he preached.

When the people learned Waltrip had lied about his first marriage, they stopped attending and Radio Chapel soon closed. The few dates Waltrip allowed her to minister alone were in places where no one knew she was married. At least once, a series of meetings was canceled at the last moment after the inviting pastor was told of her marriage to a divorced man by one of his congregation.[6]

---

[6]Buckingham, Chapter V.

Apparently, Kathryn left Waltrip in 1944 while they were living in Los Angeles, but he did not get a divorce until 1948. In one of the rare occasions when she would talk of those years and what happened, she said:[7]

> I had to make a choice. Would I serve the man I loved, or the God I loved? I knew I could not serve God and live with Mister. (She called him "Mister" from the very first time she met him.) No one will ever know the pain of dying like I know it, for I loved him more than I loved life itself. And for a time, I loved him even more than God. I finally told him I had to leave. God had never released me from that original call. Not only did I live with him, I had to live with my conscience, and the conviction of the Holy Spirit was almost unbearable. I was tired of trying to justify myself.

For the rest of her life, she frequently referred to the time when she "died," when she made the heartbreaking decision to give up her marriage and totally dedicate herself to God and His will for her life. In one of her final appearances, a young man in the audience at a conference question-and-answer time after one of her talks asked her how she "met her death." During those years of the miracle services, she talked of that experience often. She answered the young man this way:[8]

> It came through a great disappointment, a great disappointment, and I felt like my whole world had come to an end. You know, it's not what happens to you, it's what you do

---

[7]Ibid, p. 88.

[8]Sermon by Kathryn Kuhlman. "The Ministry of Healing," delivered at Melodyland, Anaheim, California.

with that thing after it happens. And that goes back again to the will of the Lord.

At that time, I felt that which had happened to me was the greatest tragedy of my life. I thought I could never rise again, never, never. No one will ever know — if you've never died — what I'm talking about. I can go to the place. It was a dead-end street. It was 4 o'clock on a Saturday afternoon. I felt I had come to a dead end in my life.

You know, sometimes it's a thousand times easier to die physically than to keep on living. . .You see, *the Lord forgives, but people don't* . . .It would be much better if you would just take a gun, pull the trigger, and kill that one rather than to take the sword of the Spirit — and this is what Christians will do. They use it, not for healing, they use it not in mercy, they use it not with compassion, but they take the Word and use it as a sword. They'll drive it in, and they'll drive it in, and they'll drive it in, and they'll drive it in, and they'll drive it in. And they'll pierce your heart, and they'll pierce it clear through. It's much easier to die than to live.

The end of that dead-end street is when I died at 4 on a Saturday afternoon. Today, I feel it was a part of God's perfect will for my life.

In one of her books, she also talked about this valley in her life.[9]

Today, I can take you down a dead-end street in a certain town in a certain state where I surrendered everything to Jesus — body, soul and spirit. As I walked there with tears streaming down my face, *for the first time in my life,* it was none of self and all of Him. When I made that full and complete surrender of everything to Jesus, the Holy Spirit took the empty vessel, and that's all that

---

[9]Heart to Heart With Kathryn Kuhlman, p. 59.

He asks. That day was the dawn of the greatest day of my life! *I had no real ministry* until I walked down that little dead-end road and surrendered everything to Him.

But watch it: the greater the yieldedness, the greater will be the temptations.

From that moment on, Kathryn Kuhlman never wavered from answering the call on her life, never deviated from the path God had set for her, and never saw "Mister" again after she bought a one-way ticket to Franklin, Pennsylvania.

Chapter 6:
The First Miracle

"I had the greatest Teacher any human being
has ever had, and that's the Holy Spirit."

*A*s far as I can tell, no one ever knew why she
picked Franklin, Pennsylvania, to begin her "comeback."
Perhaps it was because they accepted her there. From
there she went through the midwestern states and then
south into West Virginia, Virginia, and the Carolinas.

Some places she was accepted. At others, her past
surfaced quickly, and the meetings closed. In Georgia,
a newspaper got hold of the story concerning her
marriage to a divorced man and printed it. She then
took a bus back north to Franklin once again.

Franklin is in Pennsylvania's coalmining country,
located in the northwest part of the state between
Pittsburgh and Erie. Pennsylvania also was settled by
many Germans, as well as Polish and Irish. Perhaps
there was a feeling of "home" to her. Perhaps it was
simply the Lord's will to locate her in that region.

Whatever the reason, in 1946, she came out of the
wilderness and moved into the Promised Land of her
real ministry. She asked the Lord once:[1]

---

[1]Hosier, p. 49.

"Oh, dear Jesus, why didn't You allow all this to happen to me when I was sixteen years old?"

"You see, I never got tired of body then...I didn't know what weariness of body really was...I could ride those buses all night and then preach all day. All I can remember is that I didn't need sleep at all.

"Why did you wait so long, dear Jesus?"

There wasn't an audible voice...I would tell you an untruth if I told you I heard an audible voice...but He did speak to me as definitely as though I could see His Person and hear His voice: "Kathryn, had I given it to you then, you would have blown the whole thing!" And I knew exactly what He meant.

Many ministries never get off the ground, or they fall off to the right or left after making what looks like a great start, simply because the men or women run ahead of God. Some seem ready in their spirits to move as soon as they are called. Others need training and preparation time. They need to be seasoned through adversities and storms, as she was.

Beginning Her "Real" Ministry

Kathryn's "real ministry" began in the tabernacle where a great evangelist of an earlier time also began to gain national attention, and that was Billy Sunday.

The 1,500-seat Gospel Tabernacle at Otter and Twelfth in Franklin has been famous in church circles since Sunday's day. Soon after her unsuccessful tour of the South, she was invited to hold a series of meetings there, and it almost seemed as if the past eight years had never been. The burden for lost souls that she accepted at her conversion finally had brought her to a place in the spirit to be able to really do something about it.

She told a group in Washington, D.C.:[2]

I can only tell you that with my conversion, there came this terrific burden for souls. When you think of Kathryn Kuhlman, think only of someone who loves your soul, not somebody who is trying to build something — only for the Kingdom of God, that's all — souls, souls, souls! Remember! I gave my life for the sole vision of lost souls. Nothing, nothing in the whole world is more important than that, lost souls. And with my conversion, there came this terrific burden for lost souls.

. . . If all the forces of hell defied me regarding my call to preach the Gospel, it is as real to me as my conversion. It's something I've got to do if I have to stand on the street corner and do it. It's something I have to do if I have to live on bread and water. If ever you have been called of God to preach the Gospel, you've got to. If your call is genuine, if your call is of the Holy Ghost, you'll preach it.

. . . I had an older sister (who heard) that her baby sister was preaching. She got so scared. . . I got this telegram from my older sister. She said, "Kathryn, be sure you've got your theology straight," and I didn't even know what theology was. I didn't know what she was talking about, but that burden for souls, that burden for souls!

. . . (In the early years, salvation was) all I knew to preach. If the place had been filled with Christians, I still had to preach on being born again. It was all that I knew, but the love in it! I had the greatest Teacher any human being has ever had, and that's the Holy Spirit.

Not too long after she opened her meetings at the tabernacle, she began daily radio broadcasts from WKRZ Radio in Oil City,

---

[2]"An Hour With Kathryn Kuhlman."

eight miles away. Within a few months, response had been such that she added a station in Pittsburgh.

Suddenly, instead of people shunning her, she was inundated with mail; the Oil City station finally had to bar visitors from the studio, because the staff could not do its work. World War II was just over and many things were still scarce, and the station was inundated with packages of nylon stockings after she mentioned on the air that she had made a run in her last pair.

This was the time of the Holy Spirit's restoration to the Body of His gift of healing. The great "healing revival" was in progress with a number of ministers traveling the country preaching healing, people such as Oral Roberts, William Branham, and Jack Coe.

As she related later, Kathryn at that time mainly preached salvation, but she did begin to ask people to come forward for the laying on of hands for healing. She began to attend tent meetings of those preaching "faith healing" to find out more about this phenomenon of God without the slightest idea this area of ministry was to bring her international fame and help more people than she could ever imagine.

Finding Out About Healing

Years after the first manifestation of healing in her services, as we saw before, Kathryn emphatically resisted being called a faith-healer. She said, "Kathryn Kuhlman is not a faith healer. If you forget everything else you've ever heard about me, always remember, Kathryn Kuhlman has never healed a human being."[3]

---

[3]Sermon by Kathryn Kuhlman. "The Secret of All Miracles in Jesus' Life." (Used by permission of the Kathryn Kuhlman Foundation.)

Yet she always had unanswered questions about divine healing. Through attending some of those "healing meetings," however, she learned some things that it would be well for those of us ministering today to remember. She learned that "an overabundance of zeal always tends to be harmful."[4]

She said the question most often asked her was, "When did you realize God had given you the ministry of healing?" Once, she answered that question this way:[5]

In the early part of my ministry, I was greatly disturbed over much that I saw occurring in the field of divine healing. I was confused by the many methods that I saw employed. I was disgusted with the unwise performances that I witnessed, none of which I could associate in any way whatsoever with either the action of the Holy Spirit or the nature of God.

And to this very day, there is nothing that is more repulsive to me than the lack of wisdom, and I'm putting it very mildly when I say "lack of wisdom." There is one thing I cannot stand, and that is fanaticism — the manifestations of the flesh that bring a reproach on something that is so marvelous, something that is so sacred.

In those early meetings, she saw things that made her heart ache. She talked of this in the same message:

I knew how these people had struggled day after day trying desperately to obtain more faith, and then when they were not healed, they were rebuked by the fact they had not had enough faith to be healed. Having been told that if they had sufficient faith, they would have been healed, I could see the defeat in their faces. I saw that because of their lack of knowledge, their lack of teaching, they were looking to themselves almost to the point

---

[4,5]Ibid.

where they were trying to heal themselves through their own striving rather than looking to the Great Physician.

In describing her visit to such a meeting in Erie, Pennsylvania, she said:[6]

> I began to weep. I could not stop. Those looks of despair and disappointment on the faces I had seen, when told that only their lack of faith was keeping them from God, were to haunt me for weeks. Was this the God of all mercy and great compassion? I left the tent, and with hot tears streaming down my face, I looked up and cried, "They have taken away my Lord, and I know not where they have laid Him."

She spent several months searching the Scriptures for the truth about healing. Her studies in the Word brought her a new kind of faith.[7]

> "When Jesus died on the cross and cried out, 'It is finished!' He not only died for our sins, but for our diseases too," she told me. "It took several months for me to realize that, for I had not been taught there was healing for the body in the redemption of Christ. But then I read in Isaiah where 'He was wounded for our transgressions, bruised for our iniquities, and by His stripes we are healed.' I had no choice but to accept that Jesus did not die just to open the way to heaven, but to provide healing as well.

> "I knew that if I lived and died and never saw a single healing miracle like the apostles experienced in the Book of Acts, it would not change God's Word," Kathryn said. "God said it. He made provision for it in our redemption at Calvary. And whether I ever saw it with my earthly eyes did not change the fact that it was so."

[6,7]Buckingham, pp. 101,102.

Beginning a Healing Ministry

The moment when she understood that healing was provided for the believer also was the moment when she began to understand the Christian's relationship with the Holy Spirit. Shortly after this incident in 1947, she began teaching a series on the Holy Spirit in her tabernacle meetings. Some of the things she said during the first night were revelations even to her. Later, she talked of being up all that night in her rooms at the Business Women's Club, praying and reading more in the Word.

The second night was the momentous occasion often read and talked about: the first time a testimony was given of someone being healed in a Kathryn Kuhlman meeting. That was the night a woman stood up and told of having been healed while Kathryn preached the night before. Without the laying on of hands, without Kathryn even being aware of what the Holy Spirit was doing, this woman was healed of a tumor. She had gone to her doctor that day because she was so sure she was healed, and he said the tumor was no longer there. Kathryn once related what happened this way:[8]

> I listened as the little woman spoke. "You were preaching on the Holy Spirit," she said, "telling us that in Him lay the resurrection power. I felt the power of God flow through my body. Although not a word had been spoken about healing the sick, I knew instantly and definitely that my body had been healed.

---

[8]Sermon by Kathryn Kuhlman, "The Secret of All Miracles in Jesus' Life."

So sure was I of this that I went to my doctor today and had my healing verified."

The Holy Spirit then was the answer, an answer so profound that no human being can fathom the full extent of His depths and the full extent of His power, and yet, so simple that most folk miss it even today.

I had my answer. I understood that night why there was no need for a healing line, why there is no healing virtue in a card (for a healing line) or a personality, no necessity for wild exhortations to have faith.

That was the beginning of this healing ministry which God has given to me. Strange to some, because of the fact that hundreds have been healed just sitting quietly in the audience without any demonstration whatsoever. None. Very often not even a sermon is preached. There have been times when not even a song has been sung.

No loud demonstration, no loud calling on God as though He were deaf, no screaming, no shouting. Within the very quietness of His presence, and there have been times, literally hundreds of times, when in a great miracle service there has been so much of the presence of the Holy Spirit that literally one could almost hear the beating, the rhythm of the heartbeat of thousands of people as their hearts did beat as one.

On the following Sunday came the second miracle.

A World War I veteran who had been declared legally blind after an industrial accident twenty-one years before had 85 percent sight in the permanently impaired eye restored to him. He had been nearly blind in the other eye, and perfect eyesight was restored to that one. Sitting in the service and hearing of the healing received by the woman with the tumor the week before had caused 76-year-old George Orr of Butler, Pennsylvania, to ask God to heal his eye. And God did.

The crowds Kathryn was drawing to the tabernacle were even greater than those brought in by Billy Sunday, once the healings and miracles began to take place. God began to prosper the ministry greatly, but the devil tried to abort the flow of the Holy Spirit. The attack came through M. J. Maloney and others on the board of trustees of the tabernacle.

> Maloney wasn't just conducting a ministry, he was running a business . . . Maloney insisted his contract called for him to get a certain percentage of all the revenue — including that which came through the radio ministry and the mailouts. Kathryn balked. Somehow, it just didn't seem right. Maloney threatened to sue. The stage was set for a showdown.[9]

The "showdown" included Maloney's locking her out of the building, a fight between her coalminer followers and Maloney's men, and her partisans breaking off the padlocks so services could continue. It ended when Kathryn's people bought an old roller skating rink and opened a new tabernacle, Faith Temple, in nearby Sugar Creek. It was twice the size of Maloney's building and was packed from the first service.

During this hectic and crucial time, Kathryn received word that Burroughs A. Waltrip Sr. had filed for divorce in Arizona. The sheriff, who had attended her meetings, served the papers on her privately but did not release notice of the divorce to the media. Seven years later reporters finally found out about it. By that time, Kathryn's ministry could not be affected by old news.

---

[9]Buckingham, p. 108.

Services continued at the renovated roller rink and expanded to neighboring towns and to Stambaugh Auditorium in Youngstown, Ohio.

The Holy Spirit was building up a ministry that He could accomplish miracles through using someone who would not try to take the credit for His deeds nor the glory from the results of His operations.

Building the Kingdom, Not Buildings

Kathryn's permanent move to Pittsburgh from Franklin developed as a result of the radio programs which had drawn thousands of listeners in the two years between 1946 and 1948. Even at the first meeting in Carnegie Hall, that expectancy of the miraculous was operating. Although the custodian told her even opera stars could not fill the building, she insisted on his setting up enough chairs for a capacity house — and she was right. The first service was in the afternoon and Carnegie Hall was packed. She had to hold another one that evening.

After the services began in Pittsburgh, the radio ministry expanded even more. People began to urge her to move to Pittsburgh, including Maggie Hartner, the woman who became her "right arm" through all the ensuing years. But that sense of loyalty that was one of the marks of childhood and that she inspired in others around her kept her feeling committed to the people in Franklin who had stood by her and supported her.

They had taken her in and loved her when no one else wanted her, and the roof on Faith Temple in Sugar Creek would have to fall in, she said, before she would move. On Thanksgiving, 1950, the temple's roof fell in under the weight of the greatest snowfall in area history.[10] Three weeks later, she bought a home in the Pittsburgh suburb of Fox Chapel, where she lived until her death.

From this time, a worldwide ministry gradually developed. The scope of her ministry was less widely known than the miracle services which drew such attention.

In some of her messages, she would say in later years that God did not call her to build a church. Her ministry, she maintained, was not to be merged with any one building. Some are called to build buildings, but not Kathryn Kuhlman.

The fact that she *did* build churches was largely obscured by the publicity of the miracle services. However, the church buildings she financed were for other people, not for herself. The Kathryn Kuhlman Foundation, established in Pittsburgh, financed more than twenty churches on foreign mission fields with foreign national pastors.

Many called her "pastor" out of love and respect, but she was never set in the office of pastor, never pastored a church, and always said she was *not* called to a five-fold office. She walked in the simplicity of being "a handmaiden" of the Lord.

From 1948 until her death in 1976, her ministry continued to expand. All of the funds that came in went to the foundation, with the exception of a comparatively small salary. Also, she gave to a lot of other ministries and organizations. A number of ministers who are now well-known remember that Kathryn bought them their first tailor-made suits.[11]

---

[10]Buckingham, pp. 118,119.
[11]Hosier, p. 107.

Her radio messages eventually were heard all over the United States and, in some places overseas, via shortwave. For more than eight years before she died, her weekly television program was aired nationwide on CBS, the longest running half-hour series CBS had produced to that time. After 1968, her services in Pittsburgh were moved from Carnegie Hall to the First Presbyterian Church, Downtown.

Monday night Bible studies also were held at First Presbyterian Church for years. These sessions were attended by some of the most elite Bible scholars in Pittsburgh. And for the last ten years of her life, she held monthly services at the Shrine Auditorium in Los Angeles, as well as speaking at large churches, conferences, and in several meetings, some overseas, of the Full Gospel Business Men's Fellowship International, a laymen's organization founded by Demos Shakarian.

The thing that allowed her to keep going all those years, to maintain the increasing pace as she got older, and to fill her busy schedule in spite of an enlarged heart was her *dependency* on the Holy Spirit.

She Knew Who Was the Leader

In her book, *A Glimpse Into Glory*, she said:[12]

> If one is being led, then that one follows. You ask how all these miracles come to pass. They come to pass because I follow the Holy Spirit. He leads; I follow. I die a thousand deaths before I ever walk out on the platform or the stage, because I know how

---

[12]Kuhlman, *A Glimpse Into Glory*, pp. 116,5,3,4,126.

ordinary I am. I know that I have nothing. I'm completely dependent on the Holy Spirit.

In the same book, she said:

People ask, "Is this not a thrilling experience? Being chosen by God for such a responsibility?" No, not thrilling, but awesome. Sometimes so awesome I wish I had never been called. . .Sometimes that responsibility is almost overwhelming. It isn't hard work. I can stand on a platform, the stage of some auditorium, for four and a half hours and never feel the weariness because I am completely yielded to the Holy Spirit. But the burden of the responsibility drains the physical body . . .Not only do I walk off a platform fully refreshed after a very long service, but I feel as if I could turn around and do it all over again. The secret of it is this: Kathryn Kuhlman has nothing to do with it — it is the Holy Spirit. An hour under the anointing of the Spirit enables me to walk off that stage more rested in the body and mind than when I first walked on the platform. There is infinite renewal for my own body as He fills this body with Himself and His own Spirit.

In the last five years of her life, the weariness began to overcome the renewing of her body through the anointing. Those last years also brought more heartache, more stress, and more problems than in the previous twenty-five. The adversary of the Church seemed to be taking advantage of her increasing exhaustion of body to pile on stress and confusion, to harrass and hinder.

The only thing that kept her going full speed was her special relationship with her "best friend," the Holy Spirit.

Chapter 7:

Her Best Friend

**"He knows that I will be true to Him
as long as my heart keeps beating."**

*K*athryn Kuhlman's relationship with the Holy
Spirit was as unique as other areas of her ministry.
Other people over the past two thousand years must
have had as close and personal relationships with Him.
And such a relationship is possible for any believer who
will pay the price she did. However, few people are
willing to give up everything even for such a
relationship.

She called Him "Friend" and said He was her only
teacher, the "greatest teacher in the whole world."

How do you begin to develop this relationship with
the Holy Spirit? You move into that fellowship in the
same way she did:[1]

"There was a growing process," she stated. "There was
a time of learning, a time of schooling — oh, not in some
seminary nor some university — the greatest Teacher in
the whole world is the Holy Spirit. Believe me, you'll

---

[1]Hosier, p. 49.

get your theology straight when the Holy Spirit is your Teacher. I studied my Bible, oh, how hungry I was for the Word of God!"

She began seeking the Holy Spirit as a young girl.

I shall never forget those holiness campmeetings in Oskaloosa, Iowa. Oh, that's been years and years ago. They may still have those holiness campmeetings. I don't know. I only attended years ago right after I became a Christian, and before I knew anything about the Holy Spirit.

All I knew was that I had been born again. Jesus had forgiven my sins. I can remember that old-fashioned tabernacle, see the dust on the ground. Maybe I'm talking to someone who has attended one of those holiness campmeetings.

I was so hungry for more, and everytime an altar call was given, whether it was after the morning session, the afternoon session, or night, there was a red-headed, freckle-faced teenage girl who was the first to walk down the aisle and kneel in that sawdust, crying, crying, seeking holiness. Seeking some experience, I knew not what.

After one of those morning services, that red-headed, freckle-faced girl would rush to the altar, head buried in arms, weeping and crying. When the noon hour came, everyone else would leave, but she was still there. She would still be there when the afternoon service began. She was the first at the altar when the call was given again.

I never found what I was seeking there. I was that girl. I was seeking for some experience, some ecstasy. It was years later that I found out that Jesus is our holiness, and one who has the most of His holiness is the one who has the most of Jesus.[2]

---

[2]Sermon by Kathryn Kuhlman. "Surrender Brings Abiding Victory." (Used by permission of the Kathryn Kuhlman Foundation.)

Apparently, she dated her close relationship with the Holy Spirit from the afternoon in Los Angeles where she "died."[3]

Four o'clock that Saturday afternoon, having come to the place in my life where I surrendered everything, I knew nothing about the fullness of the Holy Spirit. I knew nothing about speaking in an unknown tongue. I knew nothing about the deeper truths of the Word.

. . . In that moment with the tears streaming down my face, looking up and bowing (to the Lord), He and I made each other promises. There's some things you don't talk about . . . It's like some things that are so personal between a husband and a wife. You just do not display them out in public.

He knows that I will be true to Him as long as my old heart will keep beating, and I know that I'll be true to Christ. We have a pact. It was all settled at the end of a dead-end street. And in that moment — when I yielded to Him, body, soul, and spirit, when I gave Him everything, all there was of me, I knew then, beloved, what that Scripture means: "If any man will follow me, let him take up his cross." (A paraphrase of Matthew 16:24.) The *cross* is always the sign, the symbol of death.

That afternoon Kathryn Kuhlman died . . . If you've never had that death to the flesh, you don't know what I'm talking about . . . When you are completely filled with the Holy Spirit, when you have had that experience as they had in the Upper Room, there will be a crucifying of the flesh. There will be a death to the flesh, believe me. . . there are lots of professing Christians, professing to have been filled with the Holy Spirit, who have never died to the flesh.

. . . All He needs is *somebody who will die,* and when I died, He came in. I was baptized. I was filled with the Spirit. I spoke in an unknown tongue as He took every part of me. In that

---

[3]"An Hour With Kathryn Kuhlman."

moment, I surrendered unto Him *all there was of me,* everything. Everything.

Then, for the first time I realized what it meant to have power.

She often spoke of trembling at the responsibility of being trusted by the Holy Spirit with the administration of His gifts, with the kind of ministry she had. She trembled at the thought of grieving Him. She knew, literally, that He was a person, and that the only way to be used by Him was to *follow* Him.

Trust Brings Responsibility

Many times in her messages, she warned Christians not to try to use the Holy Spirit, nor to lead Him. His power, she said, is under His authority — not ours. And she insisted that a Christian can be yielded enough to the Holy Spirit until there is nothing left of one's self.

You have to be dead, she would say, because there cannot be two wills. There can only be one. There cannot be two personalities involved. There must be only one, and that is His.

. . .There is a place where you die so completely, and you surrender so completely to Him — sometimes I could go fifteen minutes and not remember one single thing that (I) said. Oh, beloved, if you think speaking in unknown tongues is marvelous . . .I want you to know there's more, there's more, there's more.

There is a place of surrender to Him. . .when He'll take your tongue, and you become so detached from the whole thing it's as though. . .your ears aren't hearing, and *you're* learning. You're being thrilled at what you are hearing (your own voice speak). But it is not *your* mind. It is not *your* tongue. . . .

There is a place where He'll take your tongue, and He'll use that tongue for the edification of the Church. He'll take that tongue, and you'll speak with that tongue in a language that can be heard, a tongue that will bring the lost to the Lord Jesus Christ.

He'll take your mind. Do you know what it's like for Him to take your mind? I stand there only as a vessel...and He used my mind. I feel myself saying, "It isn't Kathryn Kuhlman," and nobody knows any better than I do.

...How does one know the woman over there in such-and-such a dress is being healed? I do not know. If my life depended on it, I could not tell you. I do not know, but the Holy Spirit knows.[4]

In one of her books, she warned of two extremes of the operation of the Holy Spirit prevalent in the late-twentieth century Church: Abuses of the gifts and neglect of the gifts.[5] She attributed both extremes to the average believer's ignorance of the Person of the Holy Spirit.

She also warned of temptations that come with being greatly used by the Holy Spirit.

Greater Temptations Go With Responsibility

The Kathryn Kuhlman Foundation published a little book, *Lord, Teach Us To Pray.* In it, she talked about the temptation of working for self-glory, the subtle temptations of spiritual bigotry or spiritual pride, the temptation of using the ministry for material gain. She said the secret to spiritual maturity, to being able to withstand temptation, is growth

---

[4]Sermon by Kathryn Kuhlman. "Jesus Christ Is All in All." (Used by permission of the Kathryn Kuhlman Foundation.)

[5]Kuhlman, Kathryn. *Gifts of the Holy Spirit* (Pittsburgh: Kathryn Kuhlman Foundation, 1981), p. 9.

through reading the Word, prayer, and consistently following the teachings of Jesus.[6]:

> Please do not pray to stand in my shoes or in the shoes of another of God's servants. I am very aware that if I misuse that which God has committed to me, my punishment will be far greater than the judgment of one to whom a lesser responsibility has been given. . . .

> May we never lose sight of the fact that the power manifested through the Spirit-filled life is that of the Holy Spirit, and all fruitfulness stems from. . .the mighty Third Person of the Trinity.

> . . .If ever I know beyond a shadow of a doubt that the anointing of the Holy Spirit has been lifted off my life, no longer dwelling within me, I will never again stand behind another pulpit. . .hold a miracle service. . .preach a sermon. Why? Because I know wherein lies the secret of the success of this ministry.

You will never get out of God's will if you submit your own will to His. If you ever get to the place where you do not know the perfect will of God, "don't do anything," she would say. Her counsel was to wait quietly until you do hear from the Holy Spirit, but *not* to listen to the voice of men.

Kathryn never did anything halfway. Even as a child, she threw herself wholeheartedly into everything she did — playing, working, and later, preaching. Laziness or a lack of diligence was never a problem for her. A lazy person may reach heaven, she said, but he will never amount to anything on earth.

The Lord took her "nothing" and used it to His glory. One of my favorite Kuhlman quotes is: "It isn't silver vessels. It isn't

---

[6]Kuhlman, Kathryn. *Lord, Teach Us To Pray* (Pittsburgh: Kathryn Kuhlman Foundation, 1988), pp. 101,119.

golden vessels He asks for. It is yielded vessels. The secret is being yielded to the Lord."[7]

She said, "I'm completely dependent on the Holy Spirit. There is a place in Him, a death. But remember this: Kathryn Kuhlman does not have one thing that God won't give you *if you pay the price . . . it costs much, but it's worth the price. It'll cost you everything, absolutely everything.*"[8]

Undivided Devotion

From the time she made the decision to give up her desire for a home and family for the sake of God's call on her life, she truly died to the life of self as much as anyone I have studied. The outstanding thread that runs through her life is her absolute love and dependency on the Holy Spirit.

In Kathryn's case, I firmly believe that she was called like the Apostle Paul to make Jesus her entire life.

The one thing that characterized her ministry from her days in Franklin, Pennsylvania, to the end of her life was her *undivided devotion to the Lord.*

---

[7]Kuhlman, Kathryn. *A Glimpse Into Glory* (Old Tappan: Logos International, 1979), p. 13.
[8]Ibid, p. 116.

Chapter 8:

The Glory Belongs to God

Her success was not hers but the Holy Spirit's.

*K*athryn Kuhlman always gave the glory to God. In some of those things in her life that she kept secret, there may have been mistakes in judgment, mistakes through the people around her, and mistakes through some area of lack of understanding. However, *she never allowed flesh to participate in any of the movings of the Holy Spirit,* and she never took any of the credit.

The Lord used Kathryn Kuhlman in a greater way than most ministers simply because she gave Him all the glory. Dying to self means changing your activities, changing your lifestyle, altering your desires. It means not reacting with your emotions when people speak badly of you, challenge you, or tell lies about you. If something happens and you react emotionally by getting offended or wounded, that shows there is still a place in you that is not totally yielded. Yielded flesh does not react.

Some ministers do not even try to die to self. Others are able to allow a partial death, enough to have a good meeting, then they go about their everyday affairs under the influence and direction of other than the Holy Spirit. Still others die, but then, for some reason, allow self to be resurrected. They are not able to continue walking under the total authority of the Holy Spirit.

The theme of her life was this kind of relationship with Him and the price one has to pay to achieve it. There is no "success formula," no method, no technique about her ministry that someone else can copy and achieve what she did. Her "success" was not hers but the Holy Spirit's — and she knew that beyond the shadow of a doubt.

She had no ulterior motives, no hidden agenda. What you saw was what you got. She was the same behind scenes as on stage.

Kathryn Kuhlman lived the life of a bondservant of God. In Bible times, a hired servant worked so many hours a day, then the rest of his time was his own. His money was his own, and he received a stipulated amount for his labor. However, a bondservant was totally owned by the master. He had no time, no money, no clothes — nothing of his own. On the other hand, his master was obligated to feed him, clothe him, and house him.

With a good master, he was better off in many cases than a hired servant. Jesus said His yoke was easy and His burden light. (Matt. 11:30.) However, many of God's people have chosen to live as "hired servants" rather than become bondservants. A bondservant is a willing slave bound to a master voluntarily.

Unless you are "a bondservant of Jesus Christ" (Rom. 1:1 AMP), as Paul said he was, then God does not have total authority in your life, and the Holy Spirit cannot flow in power as He wills.

Humility and Sincerity

Other characteristics of Kathryn Kuhlman that allowed her to walk continually in the supernatural include humility and sincerity.

She used to say that two questions she wanted to ask Jesus were: "Why was everyone not healed?" and "Why are some people slain in the Spirit and some not?"

She never pretended to have answers that she did not have, and she was always concerned about grieving the Holy Spirit by trying in any way to share the glory. She never operated in "hype" or in religious jargon, but she remained committed, submitted, honest, and sincere as long as she lived.

Awareness of accountability is another area where many of God's people today could benefit greatly by emulating Kathryn Kuhlman. She always was very aware of the fact that one day she would stand before the Lord and give an account of her ministry, so she made every effort to guard very carefully the anointing that had been entrusted to her.

Her humility extended even to her calling. As we saw before, she believed that she was not God's first choice for the ministry she had. She was never quite sure whether she was God's second choice or even His third choice because "the job I am doing is a man's job. I work hard. Few people know how hard I work," she said. "I can out-work five men put together. . . But no man was as willing to pay the price. I was just naive enough to say, (If you can) 'Take nothing and use it' (here I am). And He has been doing that ever since."[1]

As the Church comes into the next move of God, we are going to see powerful anointings come on people. For the past few years, an expectancy has built up of a new move of the Holy Spirit. This move, I believe, will involve people who are "sold out" to God, because it will take sold-out people to handle the kind of power that is ahead.

Qualities We Need To Emulate

Only people who have died to self will be able to operate in the coming anointing. Because of that, I believe it is very important for anyone who aspires to be part of the Lord's revivals to understand what will be required of them.

The life of Kathryn Kuhlman can give anyone willing to pay the price an example of what that price involves.

Some of the most outstanding qualities in her life — qualities I believe we need to develop as we mature spiritually — were these:

• Be sensitive to the Holy Spirit.

• Always give God your best.

• Preach the pure Word of God, and develop a hunger for the Word to the point that you are continually searching the Scriptures.

• When you make a mistake, be quick to repent.

• Allow Jesus to be your defense.

---

[1]*A Glimpse Into Glory,* pp. 30,31.

• Leave the past behind, and press toward the high calling of God in Christ Jesus.

• Yield your will fully to the will of God.

• Once you have put your hand to the plow to work for God, do not look back.

• Offer your body unto God as a living sacrifice, holy and acceptable unto Him.

• Do not conform to the pattern of the world.

• Do not limit the Holy Spirit, and give full credit, honor, and glory to Him.

• Stay aware of the presence of Jesus. Live your life in Him — walk in the Holy Spirit.

• Let love be your motivation in all you do.

• Develop a desire to help others.

• Do not be a respecter of persons, but make everyone aware that he is important to God. Rejoice over the success of others, and go out of your way to help them.

• Remember that your actions and behavior speak louder than your words. Your life may be the only "Bible" many people ever see.

• Guard very carefully that which God has given you.

• Always preach the Word, not your experience.

Her Basic Motivation Was Love

One of her biographers wrote something that perhaps sums up the life of Kathryn Kuhlman:[2]

---

[2]Buckingham, pp. 258,259.

Of course she had insecurities. We all do. She was so riddled with them that even the most casual observer could see the gaping holes in her armor. But *she was not motivated* by them, for in her heart of hearts, she was the most secure person I have ever met. It was evidenced by her unquestioned authority in spiritual matters. That was not a front. A mask. It was genuine. And when she was cut the deepest, by friends and enemies alike, even though she bled a little, at the deepest point of the incision, one would still find Jesus . . . the motivating force in her life was love . . . her love for Christ and her love for people.

When a prominent person in the world dies, people begin to look at the natural accomplishments. But when a leader in the Body of Christ dies, I believe Jesus would like us to look not only at what was accomplished in the natural world but at what was accomplished within the Body of Christ. The purpose is *not* to praise or criticize that leader but to see examples for our own lives.

Our pattern for this is the Old Testament, which Paul said was given to us (everyone under the New Covenant) for examples.

These things happened to them as examples and were written down as warnings for us, on whom the fulfillment of the ages has come.

1 Corinthians 10:11

So that is the intent and the spirit of how I have tried to look at Kathryn Kuhlman's life: to see an example of a yielded vessel. Also, I believe her life can be a positive example of what God is trying to do in the Church today.

Just as with the heroes and heroines of the Old Testament, we can see that all leaders are not perfect — in fact, few are. Enoch and Elijah are the only ones who were translated — and Elijah had to overcome fear and doubt in his life, if not other things. The key is that they walked with God. (Gen. 5:24 says Enoch *walked with God.*) I believe that is the bottom line of what God wants for all of us.

The key to "walking with God," according to Hebrews 11, is *faith*. However, those mentioned in that chapter did not begin by automatically walking in faith. Abraham's faith was not perfected until it came time to offer Isaac back to God. (Heb. 11:17-19, James 2:21-23.) Abraham did not even always tell the truth. And, earlier in his life, he was subject to doubt and to weakness in being the head of his household: Ishmael was the result.

James wrote, "Elijah was *a man just like us*" (5:17), and "You see that a person is justified by what he does and not by faith alone" (2:24). Also, see Romans 4:2,3. So *faith* and the *works* (James 2:26) that flow out of faith are the end results of "walking with God," with setting oneself everyday for a closer walk. Beyond the shadow of a doubt, that is what Kathryn Kuhlman did.

Heroine of the Faith

The spiritual maturity that came as a result of her attitude toward the things that happened to her is reflected in these characteristics:

Accountability, honesty, and integrity.

• Humility — awareness that we are the clay, not the potter. (Is. 64:8, Rom. 9:21.)

  • Steadfastness in following one's calling.

  • Hearing God and obeying willingly.

  • Lack of self-defense, self-pity, and other "self-rights."

- Consistent and intensive prayer and study of the Word.
- Dedication to the Kingdom.
- Loyalty and dependability.
- An emphasis on salvation, on the ministry of reconciling man to God.
- Trust and hope.
- Sincerity in looking to God rather than man for answers.
- Totally being a follower of the Holy Spirit and not attempting to fulfill one's calling in the flesh.
- Giving all the honor and glory to God.
- Allowing the Lord's compassion to flow out to others who are hurting.

An incident in her childhood that perhaps allowed the compassion of the Lord to flow through her to such a great extent occurred when she was three years old.

Her father came home from work one cold winter evening, having walked through very deep snow. When he came into the kitchen, he went straight to the range which was red hot in preparation for cooking the supper biscuits — bypassing his usual hug for Kathryn.

She said, "While he was standing there with his hands over the kitchen stove, just as quickly as I could, I got a chair and pushed it up to the stove by his side."[3]

When she reached up on tiptoes to hug him, the chair slipped, and she fell with both hands straight down on the red-hot stove. Her parents grabbed her, but the flesh of her palms

---

[3]"Jesus Christ Is All in All."

stayed on the stove. Her mother stuck her hands in a crock of lard and prayed, as Kathryn told the story in later years:

I'll tell you something else about my hands. You don't know how sensitive all my life I've been because these hands are scarred. These hands are not beautiful hands. They're not. . . But beloved, if He can take those scarred hands, and if He can take an old scarred life — if He can take the sinner and save that one by His grace (then He can use you just as much as He has me).

At times, when people grab my hands, and you see me flinch (this is why). These are not strong hands, but they're yielded hands. There's no beauty. You only see the beauty of them when you see Christ in these hands.[4]

Individually, and as a Body, we should be allowing the Holy Spirit to develop these same characteristics in us. They are facets of the character of God, and the Word tells us to be "conformed to the image of his Son" (Rom. 8:29 KJV), Who did only what He saw His father do. (John 5:19.) He and the Father are one (John 10:30), and He wants us to be one with Him.

Unfortunately, these characteristics usually are developed through adversity. With most Christians, it takes the pruning and polishing of circumstances to bring us into conformity with the character of Jesus.

God taught Abraham to trust Him through bringing him out of circumstances — such as a foreign king taking Sarai into his harem. (Gen. 12:10-20.) God intervened, and Abraham began to see that He could trust God as a Father, not just as a supernatural power or even the Creator. Abraham made mistakes and learned through them.

---

[4]Ibid.

The fact that Kathryn chose her own way in marriage for six years is not more important than the fact that, in the end, she chose God's way and stuck to that way to her own hurt. To the end of her life, she loved "Mister."

She said once, "No one will ever know what this ministry has cost me. Only Jesus."[5]

Another time, she said, "I'd give anything if I could have been just a good housewife, a good cook. And I'd like to have had a big family. It would have been nice to have a man to boss me around."[6]

She *chose* to put her "rights" to marriage and family on the cross, and she took up that cross and followed Jesus. How many Christians would give up even a career, or how many ministers would give up ideas for their own ministries to totally follow the guidance of the Holy Spirit?

Yet, that is the demand of this hour. God is demanding a closer walk for all who want to be part of this revival. There is an emphasis on old-fashioned "sanctification." There is an urgency in my spirit, and in many others to whom I have talked, for the crucifying of self in preparation for being raised to higher levels of spiritual maturity.

As far as our personal walks with God are concerned, it really does not matter whether times ahead bring unprecedented prosperity or unprecedented hard times: Both circumstances require total trust and faith in God as our Source, or we may fall away.

---

[5]Buckingham, p. 93.
[6]Hosier, p. 99.

Kathryn Kuhlman would have been the first to admit that she "did not have it made" yet, or that she was not perfect in her Christian walk. The only reason for taking a look at some of these unperfected areas is not to criticize but to learn some lessons. We can see some things from what had *not* been accomplished in her yet, as well as from those things that had been done.

"God was still working on her" when she went home to be with Him. How many of us could say — if He called us home today — that we have allowed Him to do as much in our lives as He did in hers?

Job 3:25 quotes Job as saying, "What I feared has come upon me; what I dreaded has happened to me." A number of times in the almost thirty years of her real ministry, Kathryn talked about her fear that the Holy Spirit would not manifest, that she would lose the anointing. She said once:[7]

> I've prayed that same prayer ten thousand times, "Take not Thy Holy Spirit from me." . . . I'm not afraid of man or Satan. But I do have one fear lest I grieve the Holy Spirit . . . There is nothing more revolting and more disgusting than the manifestations of the flesh after the Holy Spirit has departed from someone's life.

Kathryn did not want to die yet. At the twenty-second World Convention of FGBMFI, held in the Anaheim Convention Center, she said, "Never in my life have I wanted to live more than now."[8]

At the last conference in Israel, she was overheard praying and weeping, "Dear God, please let me live! Let me live! I beg you, I want to live."[9]

---

[7]Hosier, pp. 78,79.
[8,9]Buckingham, p. 291.

She wanted to live because she believed these years were the Church's greatest hour. She expected to see the manifestation of the power of the Holy Spirit in the last years of this century as had never been seen before. She saw her own ministry as a return to the ministry of the Holy Spirit. She focused on the Giver rather than on the gifts.

Something she said in a chapel service at Oral Roberts University could easily serve as her final statement to the world:[10]

"The world called me a fool for having given my entire life to One whom I've never seen. I know exactly what I'm going to say when I stand in His presence. When I look upon that wonderful face of Jesus, I'll have just one thing to say: 'I tried.' I gave of myself the best I knew how. My redemption will have been perfected when I stand and see Him who made it all possible."

Kathryn Kuhlman. . . handmaiden of God.

We still miss her!

---

[10]Roberts, Oral, "A Tribute to the Lord's Handmaiden," Cover of *Abundant Life* (Tulsa: Oral Roberts Evangelistic Association, Inc., May 1976), a quote from Kathryn Kuhlman's address to the faculty and students of the university in an ORU chapel service on September 15, 1975.

Appendix 1:

Biographical Outline

February 11, 1891:	Joseph Adolph Kuhlman married Emma Walkenhorst, Concordia, Missouri.
May 9, 1907:	Kathryn Johanna Kuhlman was born.
October 6, 1913:	Myrtle Kuhlman married Everett Parrott, Sedalia, Missouri.
Spring, 1921:	Kathryn was born again in the Methodist Church, Concordia.
April 4, 1922:	Joseph Kuhlman elected mayor.
1924:	Kathryn joined Myrtle and Everett on tent-circuit in Washington and Oregon. She was called to preach sometime during these years; probably somewhere in Idaho.
1928:	Kathryn began her own ministry in Boise, Idaho.
1933:	Pueblo, Colorado, meetings marked her first "permanent" location as a preacher. She remained here for six months.
August 27, 1933:	First meetings in Denver. Remained here five years. Began first radio programs, KVOD.

December 28, 1934: Joseph Kuhlman struck by car. Died two days later without regaining consciousness and without seeing Kathryn. (1865-1934).

February 25, 1935: Denver Revival Tabernacle established with Kathryn as founder-director. The building was completed in June.

1936: Emma Kuhlman was born again and received the baptism of the Holy Spirit at one of Kathryn's Denver meetings.

Early 1937: Texas evangelist Burroughs Waltrip, one of many visiting preachers, makes his first visit to Denver Revival Tabernacle. Later that year, he filed for divorce, leaving his first wife with two small sons. He established a work called Radio Chapel in Mason City, Iowa.

1938: Kathryn invited to preach at Radio Chapel, dedicated in July.

October 18, 1938: Kathryn and Burroughs Waltrip are married in Mason City. Almost immediately Radio Chapel closes, and the couple leaves Iowa.

1943: The Waltrips preach in Pittsburgh, where Kathryn meets Maggie Hartner, who was to be her longtime aide, for the first time. Later that year, Waltrip allowed Kathryn to preach in Portland,

Oregon, but news of their marriage leaked out, causing the meeting to be canceled. Burroughs and Kathryn moved to an apartment in Los Angeles, California. There she had her "death-to-self" experience.

1944: Kathryn left Waltrip, bought one-way ticket to Franklin, Pennsylvania, for a two-week meeting. Never saw Waltrip again. She ministered in other midwestern and southern states.

1945: Kathryn was reported in local newspaper as a "divorcee" in Columbus, Georgia. Burroughs, however, had not yet filed for a divorce. She returned to Franklin, Pennsylvania.

February, 1946: Kathryn rented Gospel Tabernacle, the site of Billy Sunday revivals, from M. J. Maloney. She began airing her messages over Oil City Radio Station WKRZ. Later, she added a station in Pittsburgh. In November, she met two widows who invited her to move in with them from her attic rooms at the Business Women's Club. One widow died, leaving her the start of an extensive collection of precious jewels and antiques. The other, Eve Conley, became Kathryn's personal secretary-lifelong confidante.

This also was the year she visited traveling "faith healers" and was disgusted and grieved over what she saw. This caused her to begin to search the Scriptures concerning the Holy Spirit.

April, 1947:
She began series on the Holy Spirit, and soon, a woman stood up and said she had been healed the night before and it had been verified by her doctor. A few weeks later, a second healing was verified.

Her business relationship with M. J. Maloney ended after a hassle and a lawsuit over his alleged percentage of the funds coming into her ministry. In June, some of her supporters bought an old roller rink in nearby Sugar Creek, turning it into Faith Temple.

1948:
Waltrip finally filed divorce papers, and a friendly sheriff served them secretly.

July 4, 1948:
The first Pittsburgh "miracle service" is held at Carnegie Hall, the first of many such services held regularly over the next twenty years. Services were jam-packed from the beginning, and miracles were seen from the beginning.

November, 1950:
Roof of Faith Temple caved in, a "sign" Kathryn had spoken it would take for

her to move to Pittsburgh. Also, she received first nation-wide publicity this year in *Redbook Magazine*. She bought a home in Fox Chapel, PA.

Summer, 1952:   Kathryn joined Rex and Maude Aimee Humbard for a series of meetings in Akron, Ohio. Dr. Arthur Metcalfe, distinguished director of a choir in Pittsburgh, joined her ministry as choir director — a relationship that lasted twenty-three years. Her long-time accountant, Walter Adamack, also joined her staff in 1952. Southern Baptist minister, Dallas Billington, of Akron's Baptist Temple, called her ministry a racket and offered $5,000 to anyone who could "prove" that she healed through prayer. Situation escalated into newspaper attacks on each other, much damage to the Church, and no one won.

1953:   Kathryn's fifth anniversary in Pittsburgh celebrated at Syria Mosque.

1957:   Kathryn Kuhlman Foundation formed with offices in the Carlton House, Pittsburgh. Kathryn, president of the foundation, was granted salary of $25,000 annually.

April 18, 1958:   Emma Kuhlman died, funeral held in Baptist Church, Concordia. (1872-1958)

1965:   First meeting in California, from repeated invitations by the Rev. Ralph Wilkerson, pastor of Anaheim Christian Center. By third service in Pasadena Convention Center, the crowds had outgrown the center. In April, she began monthly meetings at the huge Shrine Auditorium, just off Harbor Freeway south of downtown Los Angeles.

1968:   Her ministry expanded to a worldwide scale. Services moved in Pittsburgh from Carnegie Hall to First Presbyterian Church. She met Tulsa car dealer Tink Wilkerson for the first time. During these years, the foundation, among other things, donated more than 1,200 wheelchairs to Vietnam paraplegics, contributed more than $40,000 to the Western Pennsylvania School for the Blind, established student-loan funds and/or scholarships at seven colleges or universities.

1970:   Kathryn went to Vietnam to dedicate a mission chapel built with funds from her foundation, one of twenty-three turned over debt-free to nationals in Central America, Costa Rica, India, Africa, South America, Vietnam, Indonesia, Hong Kong, and Malaysia.

1971:   She met Oral Roberts in person for the first time after a miracle service in Los Angeles.

1972:   Twenty-fifth anniversary celebration of Kathryn Kuhlman ministry held at Pittsburgh's Hilton Hotel, and in May at Kansas City, Missouri. On October 11, she was granted an audience with Pope Paul.

1973:   She was awarded honorary Doctorate of Humane Letters degree from Oral Roberts University.

1974:   She was a featured speaker at the First World Conference on the Holy Spirit, held in Israel. This was one of the few services she allowed to be filmed. *People Magazine* did a four-page spread of Kathryn in her Fox Chapel home.

1975:   May 3 service at Las Vegas City Auditorium. More than 8,000 people attended. One of these services also was filmed. Later this month, she fired personal administrator Paul Bartholomew, Dino Kartsonakis' brother-in-law. He sued, threatened to publish a manuscript about her containing allegedly derogatory things. In September, she settled out of court.

In November, she spoke at Second World Conference on the Holy Spirit, again allowing her services to be filmed. However, in the months before, she attacked other leading ministers in the Charismatic movement, forcing one of them to withdraw from the Israel conference — or else she would. Three days later, she preached her last sermon at Shrine Auditorium in Los Angeles. In December, she was moved to Hillcrest Medical Center in Tulsa for open-heart surgery.

February 20, 1976: Kathryn Kuhlman died of pulmonary hypertension and was buried in Forest Lawn Memorial Park, Glendale, California.

April 30, 1982: The radio programs were terminated . . . but Kathryn Kuhlman's tapes and books continue to bless hearts and lives, and are still available through the Kathryn Kuhlman Foundation in Pittsburgh, Pennsylvania.

Appendix II:

Messages by Kathryn Kuhlman

(Author's Note: These messages have been edited only as much as necessary to translate them from spoken to written messages, eliminating repetition, and inserting proper punctuation. Any material omitted for this purpose of any length is indicated by elipses.)

Portion of a Message on the Holy Spirit:

One night I had given an altar call. There were those who came forward to be born again, but one lady, Isabel Drake, I'll never forget. She was a young lady, a teacher, commuting from Joliet to Chicago. Everyone else had gone. We turned out all the lights to save electricity. Just two were burning. Isabel remained at the altar praying.

I took my place by the side of her mother. There were not more than three or four of us there. Suddenly. . . in that moment, that one who knew absolutely nothing about the Holy Spirit, that one who knew absolutely nothing about the baptism of the Holy Spirit, that one who had never heard anyone speak in an unknown tongue raised both hands and began to sing the most beautiful thing I have ever heard.

Her voice was as clear as a bell. She sang in a language that was so beautiful — wonderful! She reached high C. It was absolute perfection. Before God, I'd never heard such singing. And her mother, sitting there in the semi-darkness, clasped my hand and said, "Kathryn, that's not my daughter. My daughter can't even carry a tune."

The perfection of that voice, and the perfection of the sound of that music! I was learning. I was seeing the Holy Spirit. I was witnessing something I had never known before.

(Then after fifteen minutes or more — I cannot tell you how long — she bowed her head. I had seen one receive the baptism of the Holy Spirit.

Remember something: I believe in the baptism of the Holy Spirit with every atom of my being. He is within you, from salvation but there is an experience with Him beyond salvation).

. . . I believe in the baptism of the Holy Spirit; but, beloved, when He speaks it will be absolute perfection. It will not be babblings. A lot of things that are called the baptism of the Holy Spirit, or lots of things that are called speaking in an unknown tongue, are not the Holy Spirit. They are a discredit to the one who is perfection. The Holy Spirit is not ignorant. When it is the Holy Spirit, it is a perfect language.

We're living in a most important hour. We're living in an hour when we speak of the great Charismatic movement. But we're living in a very dangerous hour also. Much that is attributed to the Holy Spirit is *not* the Holy Spirit. And it's this that's bringing much reproach on something very beautiful and very marvelous. There are thousands who believe that just because they have uttered a few words in an unknown tongue, they have been filled with the Holy Spirit.

There are thousands who profess to have been filled with the Holy Spirit who've never received the baptism of the Holy Spirit. You do not teach one how to speak in an unknown tongue.

John the Baptist said, "I indeed baptize, but there's one mightier than I, Jesus, who'll baptize you with the Holy Spirit." (Matt. 3:11, paraphrased.)

Everything we receive — I don't care what it is — always remember this: it's still Jesus who gives it. Everything, I don't care what it is, everything we receive must come through Jesus. He's the One. He's the One. He is even the Giver of the baptism with the Holy Spirit. Know that.

I pray the Holy Spirit shall make this real to your heart. I saw the other day in Portland, Oregon, (a little Catholic sister). She had never seen anyone filled with the Holy Spirit, never. She was in a (nun's) habit, and the power of God (touched her), so she came to the stage and very timidly said, "I've just been healed."

And I said, "Oh, Sister, that's wonderful. I'm so glad."

She turned around to go, took no more than about three steps, then she turned again to me, and very timidly, she whispered, "I'm so hungry for more of the Holy Spirit."

In fact, I did not touch her at that moment. I did not pray for her. In that moment she was slain by the power of God, lying prostrate under the power of God. No one had told her the mechanics. No one had taught her how, but a holy hush came over that crowd. I remembered something: *Noise is not the sign of power.* Always know that.

In that moment, five thousand hearts seemed as one, and all you could hear was just a holy hush in that civic auditorium, a holy hush as the very angels did bend low. That Catholic sister, who had never been taught how, found it was the most natural thing in the world to surrender herself to Him.

The Holy Spirit was healing her, and from her lips came a heavenly language. It was beautiful, so beautiful you felt like taking the shoes from off your feet. You felt you were standing in the presence of the most High. You recognized the perfection of the Holy Ghost.

I received a divine revelation that night I had never received before, and that's the reason my message to you this morning is so important, because things are happening. And they're happening so quickly. That's the reason I think it is so important that you understand that He might use you. . . .

I have said for a long time, and I believe this with every atom of my being: It's all a great restoration. Everything that happened in the early Church is being restored to the Church now — everything. And it's happening so very quickly. It's happening so fast.

This last hour all the fruits, all the gifts of the Spirit are being restored to the Church. There were miracle services (in the early Church) when every person present — it doesn't say how many were present in the service — but all were healed by the power of God.

That precious Catholic sister was being filled with the Holy Spirit, and I stood there only a couple feet from her. I was unaware of those in the crowd, absolutely unaware. I received a spiritual revelation.

On the day of Pentecost they were all filled with the Holy Ghost. (Acts 2:1-4.) (And again) there will be times, even in moments such as this, when there will be such oneness in the Spirit, when the Holy Ghost has come upon those in an assembly — those who know absolutely nothing about the Holy Spirit — that waves of glory will come upon them and every person present will be filled with the Holy Spirit and receive that baptism of the Holy Spirit. I believe that!

I want to share something that's vitally important. I do not believe that God has given me something special. . . .God has not given to me one thing that He'll not give to anyone, if you'll pay the price. I'm not special to Him. . .He'll give to you absolutely everything that He has given to me.

I would like to tell you the price is cheap. Everybody's out for a bargain these days, but God has no bargains. Young people, I would lie to you if I were to tell you that it comes cheap. You see me walk out there on the stage, and all you see is the glamor of it. And it looks so glamorous. All you see is the glory of it. That's all you see.

A reporter said to me the other day, "What do you do to prepare for a service like this" and I said, "Sir, I stay prepared."

Everybody these days wants something for nothing. You don't get something for nothing. There's a price, and it depends on what you want most. Just face facts. This generation doesn't want to face facts. . .but when you're dealing with the spiritual, it's the most important thing in the world, and you've got to face the truth.

(When I) walk out on that stage, I know what David meant when he said, "Take not thy Holy Spirit from me."

I probably know better than anyone else in this place what he meant and how he felt. I'm not afraid of Satan. I can use the same weapon on Satan that Jesus used: "It is written." I can face Satan. I can face all the demons of hell and use the same weapon on them that Jesus did. I fear no man. But (I fear) lest I grieve the Holy Spirit, lest this anointing shall leave.

Yesterday the thousands in this arena only saw the miracles, and they saw the glory, but very few of them could see the price that was paid before those miracles took place. He can take everything that I've got. He can strip me of everything I've got, leaving me but the clothing to cover my body, leaving me with the shoes on my feet, and I'm willing to go out there and live on bread and water the rest of my life, so help me God. I'll preach if I have to preach it from the street corner, but take not thy Holy Spirit from me!

If I knew the Holy Spirit was grieved, if I knew the Holy Ghost would depart from me, I would never again walk out on this stage. I would never make a pretense of things, but in that hour, I would be the most ordinary person that ever lived, and nothing would happen. I could say the same words, go through the same form, do the same things, but the secret power is the Holy Ghost.

You say, "How do you know? How do you know when somebody is healed? How do you know?"

You see, these things are spiritual. It's very hard to express them in the human vocabulary. There is a spiritual vocabulary. How can I say it to you? Only the Holy Spirit can give you divine revelation. Only He can give you the understanding (that) a place of yieldedness and death to self is the hardest thing in the world (to reach). I'm telling you it isn't easy. Death to self is the hardest thing in the world, but you can get to the place where it's none of self, but all of Him.

. . . I cannot use the Holy Spirit. I can't do it. The Holy Spirit must use the vessel. Understand something. You can have the greatest talent in the world, but it will never (accomplish anything for God) unless the Holy Ghost uses it. "Not by might, nor by power, but by my spirit, saith the Lord of hosts" (Zech. 4:6 KJV). And you become so completely dead.

You say "How can you get that way?"

I can't tell you. I don't know. I only know that Kathryn Kuhlman died. You want to know the secret of this ministry? Kathryn Kuhlman died. We talk about the death of Jesus. That was His cross, my friend. That was His cross. And the Word says to take up your cross and follow Him (Matt. 10:38).

I've got a cross that I've got to die on. Beloved, there's a cross. Jesus talked much about His cross. That was His cross when they nailed that body on that cross, that was not mine. It was not yours. That was His.

. . . A cross is the symbol of death. We don't like to talk about death, but we've got to face that. Sooner or later, in the natural, we have to face death — every one — whether you like it or not. I'm talking this moment about death to selfishness.

This is a selfish generation. It is a selfish age. People are selfish. That's one thing people never recognize in themselves. No one has ever been known to confess that he was a selfish person.

. . . I can pick up a newspaper and read anything about Kathryn Kuhlman. I can watch the telecasts. I'm not associated with them whatsoever. I do not associate that with myself. I can leave this service today and say, "Oh, isn't God wonderful?" Wasn't it glorious of the Holy Spirit, and God is my judge, in no way could I associate that service with Kathryn Kuhlman. Kathryn Kuhlman died a long time ago.

I don't know whether you understand or not. I don't know. All I can tell you is that He'll take what you yield unto Him. He'll never force you. He'll never force you — ever. If you're waiting for Him to force you to a life of yieldedness, He'll never do it. Never. And it's something you can't get out of (books).

You may know all the mechanics so far as theology is concerned. But it's something more than having the best teachers in the world. It's more. It's more. It's something more than having greater advantages than any person living. It's more than good deeds. It's something that hurts.

I'll ask one question: What do you want most in life? That has to come first. Face facts. Face yourself. Look yourself directly in the face. Maybe you don't desire what I've been talking about. Maybe that isn't your desire at all. Maybe it isn't. There are other things in life that you want more, that you feel are more desirable.

But I couldn't live if I had anything less than I have. I wouldn't want to live. That fellowship that Paul was talking about, that communion with the Holy Spirit, I couldn't live without it. I couldn't. Everything else is so worthless. Nothing else really matters, but maybe you don't want it. Maybe you don't want the best that God has for you. Maybe there are other things that are more important to you, but oh, when once you've experienced it.

You ask me why I am not weary in body after five hours, why I'm as refreshed as though I'd had five hours of rest. It's because Kathryn Kuhlman hasn't done it. I haven't done anything. I've only stood there, and I've watched the Holy Ghost do it, and I love it. I love it. I have been a great spectator, really. It's been my privilege to be a spectator to see what the Holy Spirit was doing.

I've watched Him empty wheelchairs, and I'm thrilled for those people. I'm thrilled when I see He's opened that ear. Why shouldn't that be refreshing? I'm not doing it. I have nothing to do with it whatsoever. Kathryn Kuhlman hasn't entered into the picture. When we do it, we fall apart. It's hard work when you do it without the Holy Spirit.

. . . I was born without. . . I have no talent. . . nothing. That's the reason probably it was easy for me to say, "Take nothing, and use it."

For some of you, it may be a little harder to die on that cross. That cross is there. Without exception, you're faced with a cross — *your* cross. What are you going to do about it? When you face that cross, remember: It's what you want most.

I can't make that decision for you. I made my own decision. And I'm glad that I made it. It may look so hard to you just now. It costs much, but what do you want most? That's the question. Anything else is temporary, but what I'm talking about is eternal.

So often, you know, we sing, "I Surrender," until it has almost become a cliche. Sometimes we go to so much ceremony that it doesn't mean a thing. Death is serious. Death, death. We don't like to say it or face death.

. . . Little do you know what God will do for you, little do you know. Little do you know what God will do for you, if you'll only surrender. Say (to yourself), "I die on my cross." Say it again: "I die on my cross."

Say, "More than anything else in the world, I surrender everything to you." Do you really mean it? Do you really mean it? More than anything else in the whole world? Nothing else matters. Nothing else matters.

He won't take second place. He refuses. He will not take second place, I promise you. I promise you He will not take second place. You can't compromise with Him. He won't accept a compromise. . . .

Are You Cashing God's Personal Checks?
(A Radio Message)

There's some mighty vital questions that each of us ask, and we must have the right answers. It is absolutely imperative that we have the correct answers to these all important questions.

Is God a person? Jesus taught us to pray, "Our Father which art in heaven, Hallowed be thy name" (Matt. 6:9 KJV).

When you and I pray, do we pray to a person? We must be sure that God is a person, if our prayers are to be effective. In other little heart-to-heart talks, that question was answered according to the Word of God. Yes, God is a person.

Today, we're going to continue this heart-to-heart talk by answering two questions: Is Jesus a person? and so is the Holy Spirit a person? What would be your answer if I were to face you and ask you the question, "Is Jesus Christ a person?" What is your conception of Jesus?

I probably would get many answers. The Bible says, "and the Word was made flesh, and dwelt among us (John 1:14 KJV). The hardest proposition for the infidel is to account for Jesus Christ.

Isaiah said, "his name shall be called Wonderful" (Is. 9:6 KJV), and there's no better name to describe Him. He's wonderful, for He is the world's one great wonder. No one else ever approached Him. He is in a class all by Himself. I don't care what your conception of Jesus might be, what your idea of Jesus might be, there's one thing that you have to agree upon: that is the fact that Jesus is in a class all by Himself. He has no second.

No man ever uttered such wonderful teachings. (His words were) so simple that the common people heard Him gladly, and yet, so profound that no philosopher ever plumbed their depths. He never wrote a sermon. He never published a book. He founded no college to perpetuate doctrines, but He handed down His teachings to a few poor and humble fishermen.

Yes, you'll have to agree, He's in a class all by Himself, and yet, His teaching has endured for more than two thousand years. (His words have) been translated into every language under the sky and (He) has so transformed human life that entire nations have been lifted out of darkness and degradation by His power.

. . .Who dare not agree that "never man spake like this man" (John 7:46 KJV)? And no man ever lived such a wonderful life. He backed up what He said by the way He lived. He was there with the goods. He never had to ask God to forgive His sins, because His character was perfect. His enemies watched Him like a hawk, and the very worst thing they could say about Him was that He did good on the Sabbath and let a sinful woman come near enough to Him to touch the hem of His garment.

He was born, of course, in a given race, in a given age. He had to be. But He utterly transcended His age and His race and became the ideal of every age, the ideal of every race.

How are you going to account for Jesus Christ? If He was only a man, then by every law of evolution and progress, this twentieth century ought to produce a better one intellectually and morally. Yet the world has never produced one who was on a par with Jesus Christ, even if you (believe He was a) mere man.

Surely in this twentieth century we should be able because of our culture and our scientific discoveries — and we've grown so intellectually — we should have been able to have produced a man who is at least on a par with Jesus Christ.

What are you going to do with Him? All right, I want you to see something that is more important than even His perfection or Jesus as an example. For there is no salvation, there is no regeneration, except through a person who is perfect or near perfect. There is only salvation through Deity and Divinity. Jesus Christ is a person, and thousands upon thousands will bear witness to that fact. But He had to be *more* than a person, for it takes something more than just being a person to be a great High Priest. He is seated at the right hand of God the Father, ever living to make intercession for us. (Heb. 7:25.)

Before Jesus went away, He said, "I'm going to do something. I'm going to leave you My name, and after I'm gone, you can use My name on all the checks that you cash before the Father's throne.

"I'm going to leave you. I'm going to heaven. When you have a need, and you come before God's Throne, just use My name. Sign My name on all of your checks on the bank of heaven and say, 'God the Father, I have a check here, and it's to the account of Kathryn Kuhlman.' "

God the Father would turn and say, "My goodness alive! I know Kathryn Kuhlman. Sure she's My child...You see, she was a sinner saved by My grace. There's only one name that opens the bank of glory and that is the name of My only begotten Son, Jesus Christ."

Don't you understand? You must see Jesus in a greater degree than just being a wonderful example. There's got to be more, or He could not be in position of Great High Priest. He could not be our Great Advocate. He could not be there now living to make intercession for you and for me.

When He went away, He said, "I leave you My name. Use My name, and when you come before the throne of God, a holy Powerful God, you can come before His throne and say: 'In Jesus' name, in the name of your only begotten Son, I come.' He will be there the very minute you use My name. My Father will give you what you need."

To me that's wonderful, that's glorious. Jesus is a person, but He's more than just a person. He is the very Son of the Living God. Oh, ask (the Apostle) Peter. Ask Peter, and he'll give you the answer. He was there, you know, on the Mount of Transfiguration with John, with James. They saw Jesus in a different light than thousands had seen Him as He walked the shores of Galilee.

Peter gave the account in Second Peter 1:16. This is what Peter wrote:

> For we have not followed cunningly devised fables, when we made known unto you the power and the coming of the Lord Jesus Christ, but were eyewitnesses of His glory (majesty). (KJV)

We were "eye witnesses." We were not just following "cunningly devised fables." We *know*. We saw Him in a different light than the thousands who saw Him after He broke the loaves and the fishes. We saw Him. We were eyewitnesses of His glory. We can bear witness of the fact that He is all He said He was.

. . .Oh, you could never argue with Peter regarding the fact that Jesus was Deity, Divinity. The God of Abraham said, "This is my beloved Son." The God of Moses said, "This is My beloved Son." The God of Elijah said, "This is My beloved Son, in whom I am well pleased" (Matt. 3:17).

Is the Holy Spirit a person? Now that's something to answer! One of these days, I'm going to take the entire broadcast time and just talk about the Holy Spirit, for as surely as God is a person, the Holy Spirit is a person.

Oh, I wish I could bring those witnesses, I wish I could bring Samson, I wish I could bring David. I wish I could bring some of the saints from the Old Testament dispensation.

Oh, would I love to bring the Apostle Paul and say, "Paul, is the Holy Spirit a person?"

And, oh, he'd say, "I'll tell you, He's a person! I was on the road to Damascus going to the synagogues, and something happened as I journeyed. Suddenly, there shone round about me a light from heaven. It was so powerful, it was so tremendous that I fell to the earth."

"Oh," he would say, "I tell you, the power of the Holy Ghost is real. The person of the Holy Spirit is real."

Ask those on the day of Pentecost. Ask those in the house of Cornelius. Ask those in the early Church whether the Holy Spirit was a person. Ask those who have been baptized with the Holy Ghost today whether He is a person.

But you say, "Have you ever seen the Holy Ghost? "No. Neither have I seen God, neither have I seen Jesus, but neither have I ever seen the wind. And if I were to say to you that I cannot accept the reality of the wind because I've never seen the wind, you would question my mentality."

Jesus said:

The wind bloweth where it listeth, and thou hearest the sound thereof, but canst not tell whence it cometh, and whither it goeth: so is every one that is born of the Spirit.

John 3:8 KJV

"The wind bloweth...thou hearest the sound thereof," but no man has ever seen the wind. You and I see the effect of the wind. Oh, let me tell you! We have seen the strength, the power of the wind. Oh, we have felt the gentle breezes of the wind against our faces, but no man can bear witness to the fact that he has ever seen the wind.

I have not seen the Holy Spirit, the person of the Holy Ghost, but I have seen the effects of the power of the Holy Ghost. There are thousands who can bear witness to the fact that — literally — that unseen person, that unseen power of the Holy Spirit, has filled their vessels, their bodies, with Himself. There are thousands who can bear witness of the fact that the power of the Holy Spirit has come upon their bodies, and they were healed by His power — and that His person is real.

Release From Depression
(A Radio Message)

I want you to know that I personally have enjoyed bringing you these heart-to-heart talks. I've been blessed. I personally have been sincerely blessed, because I've been talking to you about things that are very dear to my own heart.

It's sort of like opening a box and beholding a precious jewel, a priceless treasure. And whenever I think about my relationship with God the Father, it's something that is so priceless. I guard it. I do everything to protect that relationship. When I think of my relationship with Jesus Christ, His Son, it's something that is so priceless. I almost feel like whispering when I talk about it.

Do you understand what I mean? When I talk about the fellowship that I have with the Holy Spirit — that's right, the fellowship that I have with the Holy Spirit — it is as if I'm talking about a treasure so priceless that I guard it carefully. I guard it *so* carefully.

So for the past several days, I have opened my box of treasures, and we've been talking about things that are very precious, very close, literally flesh of our flesh — the most vital thing we have in our lives.

We began this series of heart-to-heart talks with a question: Is God a Person? Is Jesus Christ all that He said He was? Not only a Person, but the very Son of God? Is the Holy Spirit a Person, and during this series, we have given proof that God is a Person, and Jesus Christ, not only a Person, but this very hour (is) in the position of great High Priest, ever living to make intercession for you and for me. And today we're going to discuss the Holy Spirit as a Person.

You see, the answer to that question is vitally important. We must know that each (One of the Trinity) is a Person. It has been my desire to bring you face to face with the Person of God the Father, face to face with the great High Priest, face to face with the Person of the Holy Spirit, so that you might have fellowship with God the Father, that you might have fellowship with the great Advocate, the great High Priest, that you might have fellowship with the Holy Spirit.

I repeat what I said in our last heart-to-heart talk. A Person has intellect, emotions, will. With the intellect, a Person can know and think and understand. With the emotional capacity, a Person can feel and love. With the will, a Person can decide and act.

Now if you will, please, turn to Hebrews the fourth chapter. I shall refresh your memory by just reading three verses: 14, 15, and 16 (KJV).

> Seeing then that we have a great high priest, that is passed into the heavens, Jesus the Son of God, let us hold fast our profession.
>
> For we have not an high priest which cannot be touched with the feeling of our infirmities; but was in all points tempted like as we are, yet without sin.
>
> Let us therefore come boldly unto the throne of grace, that we may obtain mercy, and find grace to help in time of need.

All right, continue if you will, in Romans 8:14:

> For as many as are led by the Spirit of God, they are the sons of God.

Do you realize that you do not have to wait until death comes? You do not have to wait until your old heart beats its last beat. You do not have to wait until you get a new body and this that is corruption will have put on incorruption to become an heir of God and a joint-heir with Christ Jesus. If only somehow the Holy Spirit could make this real to your heart: *Now* are we the sons of God. *Now* have you passed from death unto life. (1 John 3:14.)

Never apologize for being a Christian. Sometimes I get so exercised with some of these folk who are so slow to admit — and then they admit almost with apologies — that they are a Christian, that they have accepted Christ as their Savior. Never do you have to apologize for being a Christian.

It means something to be a Christian. Know that. Square your shoulders. Lift your head high. You are somebody. You are an heir of God and a joint-heir with Christ Jesus.

If you have had that experience of regeneration, if you have been born again, if you have accepted Christ as your Savior, if you have had that transaction take place between yourself and Jesus where you have accepted what Jesus did for you on the cross, if you are a member of the Body of Christ — then beloved, you are an heir of God and a joint-heir with Christ Jesus.

Something happened when that transaction took place. Perhaps all that the one nearest to you saw were just the tears on your cheeks. Perhaps you were kneeling and praying, or perhaps you were standing there, and you looked up, and you lifted the lid of your heart and said, "Wonderful Jesus, come in."

You see, it doesn't take a long time for this transaction to take place. The very minute you are willing, the very minute you confess that you're a sinner, the very second you confess your need, He's more willing to receive you than you are to come to Him. That transaction takes place, and it's even greater than just the fact that you become a new Person in Christ Jesus. After that moment, your relationship changes so far as status is concerned between you and God. Up until that moment, God is just your mighty Creator.

That's one thing all men have in common: God is our Creator. (However), He does not become our heavenly Father until we accept His Son in the forgiveness of our sins. In that moment, the One who, up until then has been our Creator, becomes our heavenly Father by adoption. Literally, he adopts us.

Do you want to know something I found out that's very thrilling? The Lord does not permit you to disinherit a child that you have adopted.

I like that, because you see, I don't ever want Him to disinherit me: "For as many as are led by the Spirit of God, they are the sons of God." And have you had that experience? Are you being led by the Spirit of God? Have you surrendered yourself to Him? Then you are counted among the sons of God.

I am amazed how many men and women who profess to be Christians are under a bondage of fear. I can't explain it, but you know exactly what I'm talking about. And oh, what a bondage to be under! The bondage of fear, the bondage of depression, and we're finding it more and more today. . . .

Over and over again in a miracle service, I come face to face with somebody who is under that bondage of depression, and I say to them, "Let go. Remember to whom you belong." It was never in the plan of God, the will of God, that His children should be under the bondage of fear, the bondage of anxiety, the bondage of worry, the bondage of depression. Stop and remember to whom you belong.

. . . Do you really know what that means? You know, it was the greatest thrill of my life when I would meet somebody I thought was not quite sure to whom I belonged, and I'd say, "I belong to Joe Kuhlman." I wanted the whole world to know that I was Joe Kuhlman's kid. I don't know whether Papa was that proud of me to tell everybody, "That's my child," or not. But I was mighty proud to tell the whole world that he was my Daddy, and I belonged to him.

One of the nicest memories I have was when, not too long ago, I went to Concordia, Missouri, and just off the highway, I stopped to get some gas. The attendant said to me, "Are you from around here?"

And I said, "Yes, I'm Kathryn Kuhlman."

"Oh," he said. "Are you Joe Kuhlman's daughter?"

I swelled with pride. You see, Kathryn Kuhlman, the one who has preached to thousands, didn't mean a thing in the world to him. No. But I swelled with pride when he said, "Oh, are you Joe Kuhlman's daughter?" I could have hugged him. It was the nicest thing he could have said, and I said, "Yes, I'm Joe Kuhlman's daughter."

I swell with pride when I can face the whole world and say, "I belong to Him. The mighty God of this universe is my heavenly Father. I'm His by adoption. I'm a joint-heir with His wonderful Son."

In that moment when you're prone to be depressed, when you find yourself in the spirit of bondage, look up. Just pause and remember to whom you belong.

I said that it was my desire to bring you face to face with a Person so that you might have fellowship with that Person, and so now we come to the Person of the Holy Spirit.

I could never — I do not have the vocabulary — (to begin) to tell you of that fellowship I have with the Holy Spirit. He's more real to me than any human being that I've ever known in my life. Immediately — someone may say, "But have you ever seen the Holy Spirit?"

No, and neither have I seen the wind. I have not seen the wind. I cannot see air, but I am very conscious of the wind that blows it, and I'm very conscious of the air that I breathe. Without it, there would be death. The Holy Spirit is very, very real to me.

I want to read one of the most familiar verses in the Bible. Seldom does a minister standing in his pulpit on Sunday mornings dismiss his congregation without giving this one verse of Scripture, and often I wonder how many really know the deep truths found in this Word: "The grace of the Lord Jesus Christ, and the love of God, and the communion of the Holy Ghost, be with you all" (2 Cor. 13:14 KJV).

The grace of the Lord Jesus Christ — oh, the grace — coming boldly before the throne of grace that we may obtain mercy and find grace to help in the time of need. (Heb. 4:16.) The grace of the Lord Jesus Christ, the grace that was greater than our sins, and the love of God, the love of a tender heavenly Father — the one who loved us enough to give His Son that we might have life eternal. The full depth of that love we'll never know. We'll never know the love of God, and the communion of the Holy Ghost fully.

When it's so dark, we can have that communion with a Person, the Holy Ghost, the Great Strengthener, the mighty Comforter. When the waters are so deep, when you are going through your Gethsemane, there's that glorious communion of the Holy Ghost. I pray that you shall know that secret of coming face-to-face with the Person of the Holy Ghost that you might have that fellowship and that constant communion with Him.

Love Has Never Yet Made a Sacrifice
(A Radio Message)

You and I have been having some heart-to-heart talks regarding something that everybody's talking about these days, and that's love. The longer I live, the older I get, the more I realize how few people know what love really is. I mean that. And yet I know that I'm dealing with something that's vitally important when I discuss with you this thing of love, because the Word of God — and always remember, the Bible is the highest authority that man has — instructs us to follow after love.

Paul talked about the wonderful gifts of the Spirit and encouraged us to seek earnestly the best of the gifts of the Spirit. (1 Cor. 12:31 KJV.) Yet he comes to a great climax, then says: "And yet shew I unto you a more excellent way" (v. 31 KJV).

Follow after love, and even though you should be fortunate enough to be one to whom all the gifts of the Spirit were given, if you were not mastered by love, then these gifts of the Spirit would be nothing — absolutely nothing whatsoever. Everything must be motivated by love.

Love "is patient" (suffers long). But don't stop there. The Word of God continues: "and is kind" (1 Cor. 13:4 KJV).

Sometimes I think there's so little real kindness in the world today, so little of forgiveness. That's another word that's completely out of the human vocabulary. We've been adding so many new words to the human vocabulary. It seems like every time I have a conversation with somebody, especially the youth of today, I become aware of the fact that there's so many new words.

On the other hand, there are also many words being taken out of our vocabularies, and another one of those words taken out is the word *kindness.* We hear so little about kindness.

You know, once Peter — having his own theology like a lot of folks today — went to the Lord and said, "I'm telling you something. I'm having difficulty forgiving my brethren. And I've just come to the conclusion that once is all right. To forgive them twice, I can do that. I'm straining a little in forgiving them five times. I've almost reached the end in forgiving them six times — but seven times is the limit! I'll forgive them seven times, and then after that, I'll take the matter in my own hands and give them what they deserve." (Matt. 18:21 paraphrased.)

That was Peter's theology when it came to forgiveness and kindness. What did the Master say?

He said, "You poor child of Mine. Oh, dear me. Forgive him seventy times seven, and then if he's still in need of forgiveness, just keep pouring it on. Real love suffers long and is kind."

I left you (last time) by giving that wonderful illustration in what Jacob said about one of his sons.

He was talking about Joseph, and he said, "Joseph is a fruitful bough, a fruitful bough by a fountain. His branches run over the wall." (Gen. 49:22, paraphrased.)

That's beautiful. That's beautiful, and to think a father said that about one of his sons: "He is a fruitful bough." But Jacob didn't stop there. (He said Joseph was) a fruitful bough by a fountain with his branches running over the wall. More than anything else, I want to go that second mile. I want to go that third mile. I want to do more than is expected of me. More than even my Lord expects of me, for I must please Him first.

Then I want to do more than my brethren expect of me. I want to go beyond that which my enemies even expect of me. Not the third mile, but the fourth mile, the fifth mile. His branches run over the wall. . .something for the man next door, something for the outsider.

Love "suffereth long, and is kind." What next? Love "envieth not. . .vaunteth not itself, is not puffed up" (1 Cor. 13:4.) That is to say, the "ear" is never undervaluing itself because it's not the "eye." The ear is rejoicing in the brilliance of the eye. It's not envying anything that someone else possesses.

Stop right there. Don't just hurry over these things. You talk about love. Everybody's talking about love. Everybody, no matter where you go. Love, love.

There are those (hippies) today who are wearing certain clothes to try to impress upon people what they stand for — love. But love isn't just in your dress or the length of your hair. Love is something that you do. Love is never jealous.

Love "envieth not" (v. 4a KJV), and this is not only for the one with the long hair, but it's for the man in the pulpit, in clerical robes. That's another kind of dress. Sometimes I think we find more jealousy in pulpits than we'll find anywhere else in the world. Why it is, I do not know. Don't ask me! I don't *have* the answer. But very often, I think that you find more jealousy in clerical robes than in any form of dress. You want me to hurry on past that? But it's there.

You know, it would be wonderful if those who are members of the Body of Christ would realize and acknowledge the fact that we are in the same Body, the Body of Christ, that Christ

Himself is the Head and one with the Body to whom He belongs.

If someone is successful in winning souls to the Lord Jesus Christ, and he's doing more than we are doing, can we say, "Oh, I rejoice in it; I rejoice in it?"

We (ought to) stand on the sidelines and applaud because it is the same family to which we belong. It is the same Body we are born into. If only we could do that, you want to know something? We'd win the world for God. If we could manifest the love of the Lord Jesus Christ to that degree where we rejoice in our brother's success and do everything humanly possible to help him succeed — literally — the world would see the love of Christ manifested through our lives, and we'd win the unconverted and unregenerated for God.

Do you want to know who my worst critics are today? Not the man on the street, not the hippie, not the unregenerated, but very often, one who is a member of the clergy.

Do you want to know who understands Kathryn Kuhlman the least? Not the hippie, not the sinner, but the one who professes religion. Love "envieth not." That means: Do not envy anything that someone else possesses. Love "vaunteth not itself" (v. 4b KJV).

Oh, now, if you're doing something, stop doing it right now, and listen very closely. This is practical. If only you and I would get back to the Word of God — it has everything. The Word of God has all the answers. . . if man would just come back to the Bible, and see what the Bible *really* teaches, (if man would) get back again to the Word of God, the laws of God, instead of living contrary to the Word of God.

You see, that's the reason we've gotten ourselves in such a mess — because we're all living contrary to what the Bible teaches. We're living contrary to God's laws and God's rules, and we've gotten ourselves in the fix we're in today. . . .

Love that talks of loving is not love. You know, I get scared of these people who constantly are coming to me and telling me how much they love me: "Oh, Miss Kuhlman, Miss Kuhlman, oh, I love you, I love you, I love you." I found out a long time ago those are the people who will be the very first ones to turn on you.

If something would happen, (the person who helps is usually) the person who never talks about how much he loves you, but who shows his love by doing (something). They have confidence in you, they are loyal to you, they are right there when you need them. There are some folk who have never told me that they love me, never. And yet, I know that if I needed them, they'd be right there through thick and thin. They'd be right there. I could call on them night or day.

. . . I'm going to tell you something. If Papa ever had come home and said, "Emma, I just love you, I love you," Mama would have said "Joe, what's up now? What have you been doing?"

You know. . .kind of like that. (Does) that husband of yours have to keep telling you that he loves you, he loves you? Do you want to know something? When there is real love in the heart of that husband, he'll work the flesh off his bones to give his little family a nice home. I didn't say a mansion. I didn't say steaks at every dinner. I didn't say the finest cars on the block. I didn't say that. But when he really loves, he'll give his family the best that he can afford, the very best. He'll work. He'll sacrifice.

Love is something you do. It isn't continually saying, "I'm doing this because I love you. I'm sacrificing because I love you. I'm giving because I love you."

He doesn't have to. You know in your own heart that he's doing it because he loves you.

Why in the world do you think Papa ate mama's burnt cookies, and sat there and said, "Emma, these cookies are so good"?

I'm going to tell you something — the neighbor's dog wouldn't have eaten those burnt cookies, but Papa loved Mama. Mama wasn't a very good cook. I don't think she'd mind if I tell you that Mama wasn't a good cook. She was never a slave to her kitchen.

And yet Papa would say, "Oh, Emma, I would rather eat your food than Belle's best cooking, or the best dinner in the restaurant."

It wasn't Mama's good cooking. It was just because Papa loved Mama. And some of you wives can put the best meal in the world on the table, and if your husband doesn't like you, I dare say he doesn't even know what he's eating, but he sits down at the table and eats your wonderful cooking.

There's something about love, there's something about love. Everybody's talking about it, but yet, you have to go to the Word of God to really analyze love, break it apart, and see what it's made of.

Love that talks of loving is not love, and so it is with your love for the Master. (Also I wonder) when somebody has to constantly tell you how much they love the Lord — "Oh, I love Him. Oh, I love the Lord." You don't have to tell the whole world how much you love Him. Your actions will speak louder than your words. It's the deeds that you do. It's your everyday living.

It's a sacrifice that you make for the Lord — and yet — love knows no such thing as a sacrifice. Not really. That word "sacrifice" will never be in your vocabulary. It will be taken out completely when you love the Lord enough. Your giving will never be a sacrifice, never.

When somebody comes and says, "Here's a gift. Use it for the Lord's work, and I only wish it were more," I know love prompts the giving of that gift.

When somebody says, "Here is a real sacrificial gift, I hope you appreciate it," maybe they're giving it because they're pro-positioning God or something like that. You know good and well love isn't prompting the giving of that gift.

But when you can give and say, "I wish it were more. It's all that I have. It's the best that I have," God knows your heart.

When you can say, "I wish there was more strength in my body with which to serve Him. I wish I could do more for Him. I've done so little. I wish there was more that my hands could do. I wish I could give more than I'm giving," that is love!

But when you have to speak of your love, it is not love at all, for the Word of God says, "Love vaunteth not itself."

God's Practical Advice About Love
(A Radio Message)

There's something about the practicalness of the Word of God. See, to me the Word of God is so practical. It's plain, everyday living. When I say to you that I am coming into your home and giving you "old-fashioned Missouri cornbread," well, you see, there are parts of the Word of God that in my (opinion are) good old-fashioned cornbread. They're good for you. You'll grow on "cornbread." I did, and besides that, it tastes good. I enjoy it.

Now if you do not enjoy the Word of God, if you are not having the time of your life living a Christian life, then there's something wrong with you — and it's not the Christian experience, and it's not God's plan for you. Know that. Maybe you have just enough of an experience to make you miserable. Could be that. Have you ever thought of it?

Oh, have you ever seen these youngsters who are just beginning to learn to swim? ...these little old kids go to the swimming pool and stick one little toe in the pool. It's so cold, and they yell.

They scream, "Ohhhh, Mama, Mama, it's cold, it's cold!" And then they'll go back and maybe stick two toes in or a half of the foot. "Oh, it's cold, it's cold! It's too cold."

They aren't enjoying it a bit, but take that brave little kid that stands up there on the diving board! When I watch him, I say, "Oh, dear Jesus, give an angel charge over that youngster. He's going to kill himself, sure as can be." And before I finish my prayer, off he goes and into the water, and he comes up splashing water in every direction, and he yells to the other kids, "Come on in. The water is fine. The water is wonderful."

He's not cold. He's loving it, because he has given it everything he has. He has been completely immersed in those waters, and he is enjoying it.

Now if you are not enjoying your relationship with the Lord, if you're not enjoying being a Christian, if you are not enjoying these things that we're giving you from the Word of God, maybe it's because you've just gotten enough to make you miserable. Maybe you're only sticking one toe into this thing of living for the Lord. If you haven't really gotten wet yet. . . maybe you're not completely immersed in the things of the Spirit.

Oh, it's the most wonderful life in the world if you'll only give Him all there is of you. This thing of living a Christian life is worth anything, it's worth everything. It's worth giving everything that you have.

. . . I suppose if I would have a thousand people and ask their definition of love, I would get about a thousand different answers, but the Bible holds the real answer. The Word of God gives the real answer, a real definition as to what love really is. From the standpoint of literature, it is my firm conviction that this thirteenth chapter of First Corinthians is without doubt one of the most remarkable passages that ever came from the pen of man. We need to get back to the thirteenth chapter of First Corinthians.

What is the real outward manifestation of love? I still contend that love is something you do. You cannot help loving without having that love express itself in something that's very definite, something outward. There will be the outward fruit of the love that's on the inside. The next door neighbor will know it, the person with whom you work will know it, the man on the street will know it, and the one who comes and takes the garbage from your back door will know it. The man who parks your car in the garage will know it. It's something that is workable. There's an outward manifestation — if you have real love.

. . . Here's something so beautiful, and we need it to take note of it. If ever we needed it, it's today: Love "does not behave itself unseemly" (v. 5a KJV). I wish that I could get that across to the thousands and thousands who are talking about love, who are carrying the placards of love, who have thousands of words to say about love, who are having great demonstrations trying to prove to the world that they love.

Do you want to know something? We need to get back to the Bible again and see what love really is. Love "doth not behave itself unseemly." Now this verse has been translated in many ways. The simple meaning is this:

Love is always polite, love is courteous, love is never violent. Where there is hatred, you'll find violence, but love is courteous. It is never rough. Love is never brutal. Love does not go around saying ugly things.

A common expression today is "Call a spade a spade" — whatever that means — but love never says that. Love does not do that kind of thing. It just doesn't.

My Aunt Belle always told something on me. I had a cousin Howard who was just a little older than myself, and he was such a bully. Oh, he was such a bully! One day I got up on my poor little tottering legs and looked him right in the face, and I said to him — even before I had much usage of the English language — but I said, "You slap me and I'll slap you back." That was before I even knew (what) the word "slap" meant.

You see everybody's talking about love today, but those are only words. In our hearts, we're saying, "You slap me, and I'll slap you back," and what do we have as a result? Hate. The very atmosphere in which we live is not one of love. The very atmosphere in which we live is hate. Hate is on all sides of us. Love is only a word. Our actions are of hate. Yet, God's Word says that love doth not behave itself unseemly.

Oh, to get back again to the Word of God! What we need is a fresh baptism of the love of God in the hearts of American people, and not only American people but peoples of the world. We need to get back to the Word of God and practice the simple truths of His Word.

Now mark this: Love seeks not its own. (v. 5b.) Perhaps that is a profound word about the self-emptying capacity of love. Love will always think of the other person. Today, of course, everything is based on:

"What do I get out of it? What is there in it for me? What do I get in return?"

Sometimes I think that if, after all these years, Papa could return in the flesh, he'd want to go right back to where he came from, because the living today is so different than it was when he was a young man.

As a young man, Papa was a farmer. And I remember hearing him tell how those good Missouri farmers would get together (to help one another). They didn't have the modern machinery we have now, but they'd go to (someone's) house, and the women would do all the cooking — bake the pies, make the biscuits, and prepare the meat. They didn't go to the store in those days, let me tell you, to buy bread. They baked literally dozens and dozens of loaves of bread, and the men would do the threshing.

All the neighbors would come together. Nobody ever said, "Well, Joe, how much will you pay me? I want so much an hour, and I'll only work so many hours."

In those days, nobody paid a neighbor to come and help him harvest his crops. It wasn't a matter of, "I worked five hours or I worked six hours." As soon as it was sunrise, the neighbors would be there, and they worked until dark, and nobody complained. Nobody said a word."

If a neighbor was sick. . .why I've known my mother to stop right in the middle of her washing on Monday morning — and that was just about the greatest sacrifice that Mama could make, because that washing was the most important thing in her life. When Mondays' came, Mama washed.

I've known my mother to stop right in the middle of her washing when somebody would come over and say, "Mrs. Kuhlman, Sophia is sick. Would you come over right away?"

And I have known my mother to stay with a neighbor all day, all night, perhaps all the next day. We got along the best we could without Mama for maybe two days, and she'd come home having had very little sleep because a neighbor was sick.

Do we do that any more? Yet, you know, we think we are such an intelligent generation, and we're constantly talking about love. Yet there never was a generation or a time when there was so much hate in the world as today.

We're talking about something some of you know nothing about. We're talking about something that we're not practicing.

. . .Those (verses in First Corinthians 13) are all descriptions of what love does to the individual. All the way through, (the Apostle Paul was talking to) the individual in his relationship to other people. We have to live with other people. If you are a part of humanity, you have to live with other people. And the Word of God is talking about your relationship with your neighbor, your brother, members of your family, with other people. "For me to live is Christ." (Phil. 1:21.) If I do not manifest His love, then I'd better stop preaching.

God Demands Sinlessness in Worship
(A Radio Message)

First of all, in the temptations of Jesus, may I remind you that Jesus could have yielded to temptation. That fact has been established. For if Jesus could not have yielded to temptation, then the temptations would have been a farce. The whole thing would have been "fixed." The temptations would have been a mockery, and therefore, should never have been recorded.

The fact remains that Jesus was as much man as though he were not God, and as much God as though He were not man. So when He came face to face with these temptations, remember something. As man, He could have yielded to any one of these temptations.

As He faced these temptations, He was man's representative, your representative, my representative — and in the very same sense, though you and I may be tempted daily, we need not yield to a single temptation, know that.

Temptation in itself is not a sin. How often I have thought that after some great spiritual victory or after some deep consecration that one has made, the enemy is there with his greatest temptation. You and I, regardless of our spirituality, regardless of our spiritual experiences, always will have temptations so long as we are still in the body of flesh, so long as we're still here on this earth, and so long as the enemy is still with us. It's just like that.

In that first temptation, the enemy attacked Jesus in the flesh, and yet, He came forth victoriously. He stood there, absolutely perfect, unyielding, and came to the second temptation when Satan appealed to that which is the very strength of all spiritual life. He tempted Jesus regarding His trust in God — and still the Son of the living God, as much a man as though He were not God, stood there unyielding, coming out from that temptation, absolutely sinless and perfect.

Now we come to the third temptation, and the enemy strips himself of all disguise. He ceases to make use of secondary causes, and definitely asks the homage and the worship of Christ. Let me give you that portion of the Word of God. It's recorded in the fourth chapter of Matthew, the eighth verse. Remember, two temptations have already passed.

(Jesus) now comes face to face with the third attack:

> Again, the devil taketh him up into an exceeding high mountain, and sheweth him all the kingdoms of the world, and the glory of them, and saith unto him, All these things will I give thee, if thou wilt fall down and worship me. (KJV)

There's no disguise there. (Satan) strips himself of all disguise, lays the cards on the table, and says, "Now if you'll pay me homage, if you'll only worship me, if you'll bow down before me, I will give you the kingdoms of this world. I will give you the title deed to this planet. The whole thing is yours in exchange for your worship. It's all yours, lock, stock, and barrel."

What about it? Consider something just a minute. As they came face to face, they both knew that it was Satan's to give. In exactly the same way, Jesus did not rebuke Satan when Satan quoted Scripture, because they both knew he was quoting it correctly.

In that first temptation, they both knew that Jesus was Deity and Divinity and that Jesus had the power to turn the stone into bread. They both knew it. And Jesus knew when Satan offered Him the kingdoms of this world and the title deed to this planet that Satan held the title deed, and it was his to give.

How do I know? Watch something — and those of you who have been following some of my other messages will especially appreciate this portion of the Word of God because it is a proven fact that Satan was once one of the most beautiful angels that God ever created.

. . . And this is what caused Lucifer to be changed from one of the most beautiful (beings) God ever created to that which is known as Satan, the devil, today — the one who stood face to face with Jesus in these temptations that we've just been speaking of:

> For thou hast said in thine heart, [speaking of Lucifer] I will ascend into heaven, I will exalt my "throne above the stars of God.
>
> Isaiah 14:13 KJV

I think we can safely say from this Satan did have a throne here on this planet because of his speaking of "my throne." In other words, he was saying:

"I will take my throne from off this planet where I am ruling over millions of angels; I will exalt my throne above the stars of God. I will sit also upon the mount of the congregation in the sides of the north. I will ascend above the heights of the clouds. I will be like the most High God. I will have the adoration, the homage, the worship that Almighty God has."

(Always in the mind of Satan, he had been jealous of the worship, the adoration, the complete homage God had been receiving. Always, he has had an obsession for worship). That is the reason why, when we come to that period of time yet in the future which John saw on the Isle of Patmos in that marvelous vision God gave him, Satan will demand worship by men right here on this earth.

The day is coming when he will not be known as the (spirit of) AntiChrist (1 John 4:3) but in reality, he will *be* AntiChrist, Satan incarnate, demanding the worship of men here on this earth.

. . . Satan has an obsession when it comes to worship. That's the reason he takes a sinner, he takes a man, and holds complete sway over him. Men and women are (following) him who never dream that he is demanding their full and complete worship. That's the reason one of the hardest things in the world — and it can only be broken by the divine power of the living God — is the hold, the grip, the power that Satan gets on the bodies, on the lives of men and women.

He fastens a hold onto them. He demands their worship. He has such an obsession for worship that literally when he came face to face with Jesus, the Son of God, he said:

"There's one other thing. Do you see all these kingdoms of the world and all the glory? Do you see this planet? It's mine. I hold the title deed to it. God, in judgment, may have stripped me of my body, and I am left as a disembodied spirit, but He did not take from me my power. He has not yet taken from me the title deed to this planet. It's still mine. And all these things will I give thee, if thou wilt fall down and worship me" (Matt. 4:8, paraphrased).

That's the third temptation. What did Jesus do? Jesus knew the days would not be far spent before, with His own shed blood, He would have paid the price in full. He knew that again the kingdom would be regained, the planet would be regained.

He, the mighty King of kings and Lord of lords said, "I prefer to worship the Lord God Almighty. Get thee hence, Satan: 'For it is written, Thou shall worship the Lord thy God, and him only shalt thou serve'" (Matt. 4:10 KJV, paraphrased).

He came out of the third temptation the mighty victor, completely sinless...Therefore, you need never be defeated on a single score or in the face of any temptation unless you consent to be.

Dangers That Beset a Life of Victory
(A Radio Message)

Well, you and I have been having a little heart-to-heart talk about this thing of living a victorious, daily, consistent Christian life. I came to the conclusion a long time ago that "Defeat and Not Victory" is the sad inscription which could be written over the life of many of a follower of the Lord Jesus Christ.

I meet them every day. . . a long face. Oh, dear me, and there's no victory there, and there's no real spiritual vitality there, and if you are in their presence too long, you almost become depressed yourself. It's just kind of like that, and you almost hate to see them coming, you know. Oh, there's nothing worse than a professing Christian who is living in defeat.

But remember, in the riches of divine grace, provision has been made by the Lord Jesus Christ for a constant and unbroken victory on the part of every one of His children, in spite of circumstances.

Oh, you say, "But you don't understand my circumstances. If you only knew the trials that I go through. If you had to live with my husband. If you had a son and daughter like my son and daughter. If you had to put up with neighbors like my neighbors. Kathryn Kuhlman, if you had to work where I work, then you would not be able to say there is a place in the Lord Jesus Christ where you can have constant victory and be happy."

I know, my friend, but I'm not looking to that godless husband of yours, or those crying teenagers at your house, or those neighbors of yours, or the folk with whom you have to work. I'm still looking to Jesus, and you have His promises.

He said that we are not only conquerors, but we are more than conquerors over all these things, all circumstances, everything. (Rom. 8:37.)

We're more than conquerors, not through our own efforts, but through Him. Through the Lord Jesus Christ. Oh, to me that's thrilling. That's wonderful.

All right, what are some of the dangers that beset a life of holiness, this wonderful life of constant victory?

(One danger is getting into) self-effort. We can't do it in ourselves. That's impossible. We must do it through Him. He's the one who keeps us. It's not we who keep Him. Abide in Me, He says. Just rest peacefully in Him so far as your life of victory is concerned.

All right, now, the second thing: There is no freedom from temptation. The victorious life is not an untempted life. I know very often there are those who, after they have found this wonderful new-birth experience, after they've had this experience of knowing that their sins are forgiven, they feel as though they are completely free from all temptation.

Perhaps they've just gotten up from their knees, and their faces (are) still tear-stained, and I could have been the one who said to them, "Now remember to Whom you belong. You're now an heir of God, a joint-heir with Christ Jesus. He's the One. You are somebody."

And perhaps I have given them the feeling without saying so that it's always going to be just like that. There will be no more temptation. But it isn't like that. It just isn't like that. You were converted, but the devil wasn't. Sometimes we act as though when we're converted, the devil got converted too. He's just as big a rascal as he always was.

Therefore the Christian life is not an untempted life. Only one man has ever lived an unbroken victorious life, and that is our Lord and Savior Himself. And the Word of God says He "was in all points tempted like as we are, yet without sin" (Heb. 4:15 KJV). Even He was not spared temptations, so who do you think you are?

When someone stands behind the pulpit and teaches there will no longer be temptations after this wonderful experience of being born again, that one is unscriptural, for even the Son of God was tempted.

Well, let me ask you: Who are you, to believe that you have reached such a spiritual state that you will no longer be tempted?

I think back so very often. Papa always said, "It is the aggravation and not the hard work that is so hard," and sometimes I think my greatest temptation is to kind of get disgusted with people. It isn't the hard work. Preach — nobody loves to preach any more than I do. Oh, it's so wonderful, and in the miracle services, not everyone gets as blessed as I do. It's so wonderful to be in the presence of the Lord and see the wonderful outpouring of the Holy Spirit.

But you see, it's people who are so inconsiderate, and people who are so vascilating and undependable, and I'm wondering if the Lord sometimes got a little disgusted with people too (when he was on earth). Perhaps He was kind of tempted to say, "OHHHH!" The Word said He was tempted in all points as we are, yet without sin.

The sinless angels were tempted, and some fell. (Rev. 12:9.) That's right. Read the Word of God. Angels were created sinless, but they were tempted, and they did not all remain sinless. Some of the angels fell. Only one remained without sin, and that's Jesus. Adam and Eve in a sinless state were tempted, and they also fell.

So let us not be surprised when the devil tempts us. He'll do all in his power to drag us down, and he knows our weakest spots. He knows our weakest moments. He knows when we're tired. He knows when we are in a state of fatigue, and he's an old dirty rascal. He has no principles whatsoever. He has no consideration. None. And he'll wait for that moment when you're tired in body and say, "Now is my chance to strike. There it is."

Even Elijah knew that. One moment there was glorious victory. There was literally the great spiritual giant challenging the prophets of Baal and in that moment — oh, you and I think we have seen wonderful miracle services, but that was one of the greatest miracle services that we know anything about. That was a real miracle service, and I'm sorry I missed it.

You and I are in the Shrine Auditorium or in the First Presbyterian Church in Pittsburgh or New York City, and we see sick bodies healed by the power of God. We say, "Isn't that wonderful? Wasn't that a wonderful miracle service?"

But I'll tell you something. There was a miracle service that was even greater than anything that you and I have ever experienced (the one when) Elijah stood there that day, a spiritual giant, literally challenging the prophets of Baal — and God came through. He always does, and He sent that fire from heaven. (1 Kings 18:17-38.) Oh, to think I missed that one. Oh, to think I missed it!

Had I been there while Elijah was challenging the prophets of Baal, I probably would have been standing behind him saying, "Sickum...sickum...."

I would have been doing my part, I'll tell you, all that I would have known to do in the circumstances. But do you want to know something? Only a few hours later, at the time when Elijah was so tired in body there wasn't an ounce of strength left (he was greatly discouraged). He was human. He was human. And the devil was waiting for that weak moment to attack him. Just a few hours later, he prayed to die:

"Let me die. Oh, I'm so discouraged. Jezebel is out there after my head, and she'll probably get it, you know."

How quickly we forget the power of our God in those moments of despair. Did God cut him off? Did God forget him? No! He just let him sleep. He said, "Child of mine, all you need is just about twelve or fourteen hours of good sleep." Then He not only put Elijah to sleep, but he even sent the angels to bake him a cake. I tell you, that's what our heavenly Father is like, but I also want you to see the power of the enemy. (1 Kings 19:1-8.)

The devil did attack him when he was tired in body — the weakness of the flesh. There was no weakness spiritually. There is no weakness in the spirit. The weakness was in the flesh, and God knew it.

So let us not be surprised when Satan tempts us. He'll do all in his power to drag us down, because the victorious life is the only one that really counts. And every child of God will be tempted, but we can count it all joy even in the face of that temptation, for we are told the shield of faith is able to quench all the fiery darts of the evil one. (Eph. 6:16.)

That's the reason I say to you when I come into your home, "No matter what happens to you, as long as God is still on His throne, there's an answer to prayer. Just so long as your faith in Him is intact, you cannot be defeated."

Not one of us will ever go down in defeat as long as our faith in Him is still intact, and the most wonderful thing is that He will even supply the faith. Being the author and finisher of our faith, He is the supplier of that faith. (Heb. 12:2.)

I ask you confidentially — and it's a reasonable question — How can we lose? Perhaps sitting there right now you're defeated. Oh, if I could see your face. It's so long. No wonder your husband hates to come home. No wonder your children hate to come home.

Or maybe I'm talking to a backslidden preacher. Of course, you're not having any spiritual results. Of course you're not influencing your church and the members of your church. When you stand in the pulpit, they can sense your defeat. They know it, and you cannot give to anyone else more than you have experienced yourself.

How can you give someone else victory when you have no victory yourself? You can't do it. It's the life of victory that is the only one that really counts, and you can look up, having the shield of faith. That shield of faith, regardless of circumstances, is able to quench all, *all,* the fiery darts of the evil one. If it wasn't true, God's Word never would have said it.

There are those who say, "Now if we fall, what?"

There are people that sometimes I think are actually born with negative attitudes. When they make their first cry, it's a negative cry, and they go through life still crying negative tears. Everything they say, and all their thoughts are negative.

If we fail."

"I'm afraid to accept Christ as my Savior because maybe I'll not be able to live the life."

Don't ever say that to me, whatever you do! I may show some of the human side of me. That's one thing I cannot take from anybody! When they give (these words) as an excuse, "Maybe I won't be able to live the life. Maybe I won't be able to hold out. If we fail...."

There's always the possibility of sinning, but remember, Jesus knew the weakness of the flesh. He created us. He knows all about us. He knows us better than we know ourselves. And so He has made a provision for this possibility of sinning. Oh, He's a wonderful heavenly Father.

Go back if you will, please, to the Old Testament to the fourth chapter of Leviticus, and verse 3 (KJV) says, "If the priest that is anointed do sin according to the sin of the people" — look at that!

You say, "My goodness. I never thought of a priest sinning."

Well, God did, the Creator did. Always keep in mind, there's only one who was sinless, just one. A person can be deeply spiritual, yet that person is not immune to temptation. God knew it. If the priest that is anointed, if that priest do sin as the people, what happens? He has to confess that sin just like anyone else, because he's a human being, too. Now doesn't this prove that sin is inevitable? Now watch.

Every ship that sails is provided with a supply of lifeboats, lest there should be a wreckage or a collision. Every ship — I don't care how small, how large — is always provided with lifeboats, because there's always the possibility of a storm. There could be a shipwreck, and of course, this does not imply that it is the captain's intention to wreck his ship nor does it mean that every ship must be wrecked. No. But if we confess that sin — "he is faithful and just to forgive us" (1 John 1:9 KJV).

Confession is one of the most important doctrines, one of the most important things, of man's theology and of God's Word. There must be confession, and you confess your sins to Him. Oh, I know. You see, the enemy of our soul who is the accuser of the brethren, will keep attacking you on this one score.

He will say, "Ah ha, you did it. You did it. You yielded. You did it. In that moment of weakness, you did it."

He's the accuser of the brethren. Don't act like the devil, now, whatever you do.

Jesus said, if we confess, if we sin — whether we be priest or just an ordinary person — He's made a way, a provision through His tender love, and He is there to forgive us of that sin.

Bibliography

A Legacy. (Pittsburgh: Kathryn Kuhlman Foundation.)

Buckingham, Jamie. *Daughter of Destiny* (Bridgeport: Logos International, 1976).

Hosier, Helen Kooiman. *Kathryn Kuhlman* (Old Tappan: Fleming H. Revell Company, 1976).

"Kathryn Kuhlman, 25 Years in Pittsburgh," *Logos Journal.* November-December, 1972.

"Kathryn Kuhlman in Las Vegas," *Logos Journal,* July/August, 1975.

Kathryn Kuhlman Interview: "Healing in the Spirit," *Christianity Today,* July 20, 1973, pp. 1076-1082.

"Kuhlman Had No Successor," *Dallas Morning News,* March 26, 1977.

Kuhlman, Kathryn. *Gifts of the Holy Spirit* (Kathryn Kuhlman Foundation, 1981).

Kuhlman, Kathryn. *Heart-to-Heart With Kathryn Kuhlman* (Pittsburgh: Kathryn Kuhlman Foundation, 1983).

Kuhlman, Kathryn. *How Big Is God?* (Minneapolis: Bethany Fellowship, Inc., 1974).

Kuhlman, Kathryn. *Lord, Teach Us To Pray* (Pittsburgh: Kathryn Kuhlman Foundation, 1988).

Kuhlman, Kathryn. *I Believe in Miracles* (Prentice-Hall, Inc., 1962).

Kuhlman, Kathryn. *10,000 Miles for a Miracle* (Bethany, 1974).

Kuhlman, Kathryn with Buckingham, Jamie. *A Glimpse Into Glory* (Logos International, 1979).

Logos Journal. November/December, 1976.

The Oracle. Oral Roberts University, Tulsa, Oklahoma, September 26, 1975.

Spraggett, Allen. *Kathryn Kuhlman, The Woman Who Believed in Miracles* (New York: New American Library, 1970).

"Oral Roberts' Tribute to the Lord's Handmaiden," *Abundant Life Magazine.* Oral Roberts Evangelistic Association, Inc., May, 1976.

Other Books by Roberts Liardon

Run to the Battle

Learning To Say No Without Feeling Guilty

I Saw Heaven

Success in Life and Ministry

The Invading Force

The Quest for Spiritual Hunger

The Price of Spiritual Power

Breaking Controlling Powers

Religious Politics

Cry of the Spirit

New From Harrison House

Spiritual Timing

Videos by Roberts Liardon

The Lord Is a Warrior

I Saw Heaven

Stirring Up the Gifts of God

God's Generals

8-volume set of tapes, 60-minutes each

Available from your local bookstore
or by writing:

Harrison House

P.O. Box 35035 • Tulsa, OK 74153

Roberts Liardon was born again at the age of eight years, baptized in the Holy Spirit, and called to the ministry after being caught up to Heaven by the Lord Jesus.

Roberts was powerfully commissioned by the Lord to study the lives of God's great men and women ministers, to know why they succeeded and why they failed.

At age fourteen, Roberts began preaching and teaching in various churches — denominational and non-denominational alike, Bible colleges, and universities. He has traveled extensively in more than 30 nations over the past few years. Roberts' missions outreaches have taken him through the United States and to Canada, Africa, Europe, and Asia. Many of Roberts' books have been translated into foreign languages.

Roberts ministers under a powerful anointing of the Holy Spirit. In his sermons, Roberts calls people of all ages to salvation, holiness, and life in the Holy Spirit.

To contact the author,
write:

Roberts Liardon
P. O. Box 23238
Minneapolis, MN 55423

Please include your prayer requests
and comments when you write.

The Harrison House Vision

Proclaiming the truth and the power
Of the Gospel of Jesus Christ
With excellence;

Challenging Christians to
Live victoriously,
Grow spiritually,
Know God intimately.